VOYAGING THROUGH TIME

PATRICIA HANN

Published by BookPublishingWorld 2021

Copyright © Patricia Hann 2021

All rights reserved. No part of this publication may be reproduced, stored in a retrieval system, or transmitted in any form or by any means, electronic, mechanical, photocopy, recording or otherwise, without prior written permission of the copyright owner. Nor can it be circulated in any form of binding or cover other than that in which it is published and without similar condition including this condition being imposed on a subsequent purchaser

ISBN: 978-1-8384967-0-8

Published by
BookPublishingWorld
An imprint of
DolmanScott
www.dolmanscott.com

For Audrey Judge and the friendship of a lifetime

As If

To Audrey whose woodcut has supplied our illustration

As if, after the late mists, wilting away of leaves,
gales that brought the tiles down, stripped the magnolia bare,
sky gone grey and heavy, beds blanked out with snow,
this was a time to venture, the bulb put out its green
exuberant enterprise. Soon a snowdrop was there.

As if, after the long entire suspension of things,
cocooned in darkness, on a dark regimen
dwindling to insect, now that the call has come
to a different order, time could begin again,
breaching a last membrane, the moth tries out her wings.

As if, after the blow that fell, the year's stillness,
ash laid to rest beneath the lilac you loved,
Time would give back our closeness that he took -
see, now we have your apposite woodcut
that completes, graces, almost names this book.

Patricia Hann was born in 1924. She lives in the Royal Borough of Greenwich, London

FOREWORD

This poetry collection presents a patchy record of an almost hundred-year-long life as it was lived until Covid 19 came into view. There is no mention of World War 2, which I lived through mainly as an evacuee and wrote about only in letters, and there is no mention of Covid in the poems, only one of which was written later than 2018. But, reading through what I have written over the years, I can almost catch a sense of the pandemic waiting in the wings. The growing experience of crowding everywhere, the mass production methods of stock rearing, the human crowding out of wildlife, plant and animal, and the prospect cheerily propounded by extreme technology of emigration to another planet when depletion and pollution will have rendered this one uninhabitable - all this was making for an unhealthy state of things. At the same time, I am not one to underrate the many benefits we enjoy from our advanced technology, as well for some of the changes it has brought to our way of living as for the enlargement of our understanding both of the world we live in and of what may be beyond. But the first function of poetry is to entertain, and I hope there are poems here that will do that.

Contents

FOREWORD vii

GOING THROUGH THE STAGES 1
   Blacking the Range 3
   "Backward" 4
   Noises in the Night 5
   A Grandpa 6
   The Spool Runs Back 8
   Telling the Time 9
   My Father's War 10
   Work 11
   A Tale of Mud 12
   Cinema of the Thirties 13
   Trafalgar Square 14
   Look At It This Way 15
   Under the Clock 16
   Heart's-Ease 17
   Prayer for Hallowe'en 18
   A Door Onto The Street 19
   Floribunda 20
   Sonnet for a Stranger 21
   No Flowers 22
   Not a Letter 23
   Poetry He Said 24
   Another Autumn 25
   Gifts From The Garden 26
   Rainy Day In The Strand 27
   Sunday Afternoon Walk 28
   "Woman Reading" 29
   End of the Line 30
   Series Discontinued 31
   The Headland 32
   Sisters in a Wood 33

Ice 34
No Transmission 35
The Old Man Comes For Christmas.. 36
Trafalgar Ward, Greenwich D.H.. 37
An Inhospitable Place 38
The Possessor of a Toothpick 39
The Ever Gracious Minister 40
Going To The Polls 41
Talking of Travel 42
Tracking Down 4B 44
Voyage of Discovery 45
Unremarkable Day.. 46
A Celebration: for A.J... 47
Three Birthday Poems 48
For Audrey in May 48
Birthday Poem for Audrey... 48
Most of All.. 49

GREEN AND PLEASANT LAND 51
A Home... 53
Encounter... 55
New Neighbour 56
To a Blue Butterfly 57
Frog In Ivy.. 58
Jays on the Lawn 59
Spring In The City 60
In a Summer Garden.. 61
In Praise Of Summer 62
Under The Leaves... 63
Islands... 64
A Horticultural Question 65
Autumn Takes Over.. 66
Winter Coming 67
Robin and Rake 68

Zero 69
In Time Of Elm Sickness 70
Owls 71
The Touch of Earth 72
Water in its Phases 73
The Sea 74
Into the Depths 75
Grass 76
A Tree 77
Climbing Cader Idris 78

SOME PORTRAITS 81
Which Portrait Painter? 83
Identities 84
A Question for Descartes 85
George Claessen Nearing Ninety 86
Millbank Steps 87
Anniversary 89
Exit a Princess 91
In Aunt Mona's House 92
Dialogue with Plum Tree 93
He Comes Back 94
Remembering B.W. 95
A Late Friendship 96
Rooster 98
For An Australian Visitor 100
Intoxications 101
Clothes 102
Funny Hat 103
Visitation 104
A Voice Goes Missing 106
Emeritus 107
The New Endymion 108
A Very Ordinary Life 110

Moonlight 112
Coniston Water 113
The Lady Talks 114
Alcestis - The Inside Story 115
Return to Ithaca 118
She Questions Him 120
Voice From The Labyrinth... 121
The Minotaur Explains 122
Unicorn 123
The Unicorn Speaks 124
Here Be Dragons 125

THE WORLD WE LIVE IN AND BEYOND 127
A Bus Journey.. 129
A Faint Celebration of London.. 130
Incident on a Train... 131
Keeping an Eye on the Thames 132
Seeing in the Year 133
Kills 99%.. 134
How Things Got This Way 135
The Aged - A Solution 136
Return of the Comet 137
Science Will Tell You 138
Life History Of Stones... 139
Creation and After 140
Origin.. 142
Space Is The Playground Of The Illusionist......................... 143
Rainbow.. 144
The Snake's Version 145
The Wrong Kind of Apple 146
What Now?... 147
The Takeover 148
How To Be God - Just The Basics 150
Off the Record 152

Announcement	155
Dinosaur	157
A Fishy Theory	158
How To Know Vampires	159
A Letter To The Angel Of The North	160
Hermit Wanted	161
The Great Leap	162
The Snowdrop's First Assignment	163
The Sad Case Of The Fractals	164
Horace Updated	165
Index of Titles	166

GOING THROUGH THE STAGES

Blacking the Range

Not many remember the old black kitchen range
with fire skulking or raging behind bars
heating the adjacent oven and the fierce hob
where kettles seethed and simmered, sometimes spat,
waiting until hot water should be needed.
And toast made at the end of a long fork
was burnt in stripes from the imprint of the bars.

Those ranges needed blacking, and my mother,
a bookish child, was kept home for such chores.
The second brush (the one for burnishing)
was worn half bald already but she worked on,
dreaming of fairy godmothers and a doll,
dimpled and curled, she'd gazed at in the window
till her mother told her she was a Big Girl now.

But one day, she recalled, her mother came home
and setting down her shopping said quite kindly,
"There's something in there for you." It wouldn't have done
to jump about or show too much impatience
or hazard guesses or seem to want to rush
the unpacking and putting away of item after item
until the last. It was a new blacking brush.

"Backward"

He gave no answers, and he never stayed
like everybody else trapped at a table,
but when he tired of sums and scripture stories,
or merely of being himself, would slither down
from his seat and stalk about the room on all fours.
He was a bear perhaps or the wolf that was going
to bolt the seven kids, through a wilderness
where all the trees were legs. Nobody stopped him.

Primly deploring, we would watch the scandal,
the lawlessness. Did any law apply
beyond the frontier of that reservation
where dumbly he retired, always alone?
Immune he did what's never to be done.
A nerve twitched; something still preserved us rigid.
Dimly we longed, and feared, to be like him.

Noises in the Night

That dark man was my grandpa, she would tell me.
He did some things she never knew about.
By day you wouldn't see him move a muscle
or hint at anything he might have thought.

Nights were another matter. We'd be tucked up
in the brass fourposter they had always slept in,
and then would come these eerie whistling noises
at odd times in the night. What were they meant for?

Trust a grownup to reason things away. I
must just have dreamt it all, although I hadn't.
Was there some game afoot that might explain why
she had to be asleep for it to happen?

But he showed the same set face every morning
still watching from his mantelpiece, unwinking.

A Grandpa

I never had a grandpa of my own,
but Marian's grandpa had been good to me.
He gave me a two-tiered wooden pencil-box,
the sort that big girls had, with flowers on top
and a special place where you could put the rubber.
And once he gave me a deep-red rose, so perfumed,
so cool and clear, perfect in every petal,
that I thought "beauty" and sensed what the word meant.
And he said I ought to kiss him but I wouldn't.

He lived in a house with a curtain over the door
and a grey parrot that said, "Goodbye, come back soon."
He had an allotment where he grew some green things
on the other side of the fence, and when he worked there
his wife would call "Coo-ee!" across the allotments,
he'd coo-ee back and go home to his dinner.

But then one day when I was on my own
he knocked and asked to come in from the rain,
and made me sit on his knee although the sofa
had plenty of room on it for both of us.
I didn't like his beard. And then the rain stopped.
He went then, saying, "No need to tell your mother
that I came in the house." That made me wonder.
So when I was saying what had happened that day
I asked why shouldn't I have told my mother.
And then they told him never to come again,
and told me I must never speak to him,
not even to say I couldn't. Strange thing with grownups -
you'd never know how they were going to take things.

Next time he passed the house I signed goodbye
and that I mustn't speak. He only said,
"I told you not to tell." And well, you see,
I never had a grandpa of my own.

The Spool Runs Back

I was in disgrace. Why wouldn't I dance for Aunt Julie
who was always so good to us? And when they forced me
why could I think of nothing by way of dance
but mimicking the moves of my little sister?
It was rude and wicked, a searing black transgression.

Next day the spots came out and resolved the question;
the spool ran backward, yesterday unhappened.
Those misdeeds weren't my doing; chickenpox did them.
Who'd dream the slate could be wiped clean like that?
Since then, at every crime brought home to me
I've looked for chickenpox, for the spool to wind back.

Telling the Time

A child in the twenties knew if you said, "Can't"
grownups would snap, "There's no such word as *can't*"
(though there was for them, which must be how we'd heard it).
And as for "Won't", only bad children said that.

So when I was sent from class into the hall,
where the big clock was, to find out the time,
I went into the hall where the big clock was
and stood there gazing up, as a votary
of Diana might stand gazing at the moon.

I thought out what to do. I knew the numbers,
and my mother had a great big cardboard clock
with hands you could move; she'd shown me how to read
half past and quarter past, and I knew with real clocks
you only had to wait till the hands came round
and it would be a quarter past or half past.

It did mean waiting, and the buzz of a lesson
behind the partition went on, and now and then
someone came through the hall, but no-one asked me
what I was doing out there, and the hand was moving,
very slowly, but I knew it must come round
and I could go back and say,"It's half past ten."
It meant I could tell the time. Some children couldn't.

But before that someone came across the hall
and took me back into the class I'd come from.
I thought they would be cross, but they said nothing.

My Father's War

The songs he sang were songs he used to march to,
about an old kitbag or dear old Blighty
or Tipperary or Armentières. And some days
he'd tell about the war. The hole in his back
was drilled by shrapnel. Some lost arms or legs.
I pictured sawdust seeping from hurt dolls.
The wounded on the streets had all been sewn up.
A lot were dead, but what was being dead like?

A German gasmask he'd picked up somewhere,
goggle-eyed, with trailing snout, showed just how gruesome
Germans must be. And there was some metal plating
ripped from a shattered plane, where he'd scratched war scenes,
planes falling, exploding bombs, tanks, soldiers running,
both arms in air. A far, strange world it seemed.
War was a nasty business, my father said;
he'd never fight another, no power should force him.
(But that last one had been a war to end wars.)

Work

My father lit the fire on winter mornings.
He chopped the wood, and made things out of wood -
my mother's footstool, bookrest and woolwinder
and the great airer in the kitchen you could
haul up and down on pulleys. And the tea-trolley
that broke one day when we took rides on it.
My mother's rich cousins had to admit
he could be just the man to be marooned with.

I'd watched him measuring, pencilling, planing, sawing
and banging the nails in, when the door was open
in the great shed he'd put up in the garden -
a place of sharp tools, guarded with a padlock.
There he would work after we'd gone to bed,
and once kept secret right till Christmas morning
a wondrous painted see-saw. I had seen
the triumph and the mastery of these things.

So when in school they spoke of Joseph's trade
I saw my father's shed and the desk he'd made me
with a real inkwell and space under the lid
to keep my secret scrawls safe from my sister.
But I was stunned that night to hear him say,
"Whatever made you tell them I was a carpenter?"
I thought he'd have been proud of all he'd made,
but he seemed piqued. "That's not my *work*," he said.

A Tale of Mud

My mother said it was because he was kind
she married him. But kind men generally
stay poor, and kindness spreads itself so wide,
no telling where the end of it will be.

And there was that day, walking to the beach,
we passed a huddle of tiny fish that writhed
and stifled in a shallow swampy patch.
It must have been a pool before it dried.

My dad, who'd seen a more commodious spot
quite near at hand, took my toy pail and went
down in the mud, prepared to set about
the delicate task of fish resettlement.

My mother thought he had no call to do it;
those fish were strangers, barely flesh and blood.
Besides, his shoes would certainly be ruined
standing about so long in all that mud.

When Raleigh flung his cloak down in the mire
he might have guessed the queen'd reciprocate.
My father thought of nothing else but how
he couldn't leave those fish to suffocate.

Sir Walter's flamboyant gesture is a legend
historians in every age rehearse.
My father's deed soon no-one will remember;
that's why I need to set it down in verse.

Cinema of the Thirties

Flawless complexions - film stars all had those:
Lux toilet soap (or was it Knight's Castile?).
Flawless the tears (of glycerine) that rose
for every noble passion they must feel.
This was true life as it was meant to be;
our sniffling sobs in the stalls were grossly real.

Elegant, and uncreased, their night attire
when William and Myrna were aroused from bed
where they'd been sleeping sound (need you enquire?)
That question never raised its ugly head.
And always (out of shot) each of the pair
must have one foot on the floor, Lord Chamberlain said.

Most were unmarried, though, destined to rise
to the long-awaited climax of a kiss
chaste as the flutterings of butterflies,
signalling unadulterated bliss.
When I was growing up that's how it was;
what nice girl would have wished it otherwise?

All I can say is, life was a surprise.

Trafalgar Square

The idea was my father's. Christmas lights.
Carols. Something neither would have thought of.
But we were on our own now, apt to drift.
The tall pine from Norway glittered like a bride
and the exuberant fountains went on playing,
but it was an absence we were standing in.

Her needles would click in and out of the stitches
as she read from the folding bookrest he had made her.
That was her leisure. At night we'd hear the treadle
of her Singer stitching the clothes we'd soon be wearing.
But uniform for the new school, how to find it
to fund those chances she had been denied?
Pounding her Remington, she'd defy hard times.

Omniscient as God but more focused,
she was the giant figure on my skyline
but had no spell to beat time's ravages off.
Still, dying was not her style. The fabled Reaper
should have quailed before her, as I quailed that time
she said, Look at me. Where did you get this thimble?
and made me take it back. When her end came
I thought, But how could she have let this happen?

That night in the Square comes back to me, the chill,
the lights, the festive noises surging round us,
our strange selves questioning the life to be,
two skiffs torn from their moorings to go free.

Look At It This Way

They embraced just once, thanks to a handy ladder,
then died, in verse, and young. What could be sadder?

And what more certain than their star's defection
to enshrine young love in all its sweet perfection.

No squalling offspring ever wrecked their nights
or sent him straying after fresh delights.

He never snored, she never burnt the cooking
or sighed, then looked to see if he was looking.

They never lost their teeth, or hair, or sweetness,
or breakfasted in less than perfect neatness.

Perfection takes long labour to rehearse;
Verona's lovers still embrace, in verse.

Under the Clock

"I may be late," he said:
"ice, fog on the line -
it could be any time.
I'll ring you. Don't you wait."

She laughed. "Don't mind the time,
look for me just the same
under the clock," she said.
"I'll wait all my life."

Vows uttered are the wild
grain of eternities.
Whatever fades or dies,
their passionate impulse lives.

Ice, fog on the line
made a ghost of him.
Out of the autumn gloom
his shadow floated wide,

failing that darker one
under the clock, that waits
caught in the sepia haze
of an endless afternoon.

Heart's-Ease

"They are called heart's-ease," you said,
the diminutive yellow pansies
breasting the pale stubble in the fall of the year.
So this was heart's-ease! I had heard the name.

The sun rode high in the wide
blue expanse; flotillas
of white cloud lay becalmed on the clear air.
No traffic seared the silence - tractor or plane.

From the fenced-in private wood
where no-one goes but trespassers
drifted rhythmically the craarks of the rooks there.
The sound meant happiness, both felt the same.

Far away the world sped
past the fields and the hoarse rookeries
where we found the small shy pansies, the first that year.
This was heart's ease. I'd always known the name.

Prayer for Hallowe'en

These have not stooped to sip shuddering on Lethe's brink
from the lullaby languid water some say the dead drink
but burning to frequent old haunts, old loves, have come
from traceless tracts beyond oblivion.

Hollow-eyed, hollow-skinned, unsinewed, paper-
thin marionettes jerked free from time's long torpor,
here they skulk on dark stairs, loll their weightless heads
in empty doorways snuffing the warmth of homesteads.

Tomorrow to be exorcised with parsonical words of blessing,
tonight, shadowy presences, you are mutely in possession.
Then, whether you came to bless or to envy and reprove,
look mildly, kindly on us and our warm love.

A Door Onto The Street

Long ago when I lived in the land of horn-dancers
the cottage living-room opened onto the pavement.
There were no numbers but if you named the person
the locals would point out the house you wanted.

On shivery ash-grey mornings they'd proclaim,
"A grand day!" if it wasn't downright raining.
The village and "the college" were distinct tribes
divided by damp-courses and piped water

and writing letters home and a nicety
about peering in through windows. An old man once
glaring in at my paintpot and ladder, growled,
"That is no occupation for the Lord's day."

My poor dog, too, would howl like a lost soul
when church bells rang out. And my fruit bowl brought
small boys to stare and sigh. "I wish I had
one of them grapes." *One!* I made for the door ...

But what if they started and took off like thrushes,
fearing some sour reward for coveting?
Or were offended? Or if hoping for more they
should come back every day? And I did nothing.

Floribunda

At the edge of the garden the jubilant red floribunda
has burst through the paling to straddle the path on the hill.
As I stand at the window musing on this and on similar
garden truancies, morning is streaked with the shrill

predations of children - three or some four of them
half out of sight in the leaves, where a hand comes round,
and another, impatient to seize on the treasure-trove roses -
impudent as sparrows. And I think how I might confound

by some slight unconsidered sound or movement
this improbable moment of Arcadian innocence
as I stand at the uncurtained window, invisible
as a ghost at daybreak and of less consequence,

and, like a ghost, inhabiting half some bygone vividness,
where I ran down glad to the glistening garden in early dew
for the roses, and half welcoming the cheerful pillaging.
Who is there now that I should give them to?

Sonnet for a Stranger

Not a grain of this body knows you, or could know -
all perished, disintegrated, dissolved in air,
recycled like old rags, whatever of us was there
when we looked, listened, laughed, those years ago.
We are made over new, or nearly so;
replacement cells take on the wear and tear
like new brash servants callously unaware
of the old house in its heyday and morning glow.

If then these entities, changed utterly -
these slowly updated replicas of us - should
come face to face murmuring a timeworn name,
by what inscrutable spontaneity
could recognition spark, smiles start? Then would
hand reach for hand, thinking themselves the same?

No Flowers

Then I rang off. And now, deep in the stillness
resounds the slamming of a distant door
known once, that will not open any more.
So you, my dear, have gone the first to rest,
and all those days - that's an old story finished
long years before.

The church still stands where they must congregate,
friends, children, children's children, row on row,
all ceremonious, where you lie and wait.
I shall not go.

Flowers? Send flowers - armfuls of daffodils
(the first flowers you gave me). They'd rise and gleam
among the hymn books and the grim paraphernalia,
tall as a dream.

But if I were to thrust an arm in there
in that familial pious company
with my bold yellow trumpets, how they'd stare,
then read the name on the card: *But who is she?*
No, better let it be.

Not a Letter

Our first spring without letters.
I didn't write for your birthday,
I didn't tell you how the crocuses
took off this year and colonised half the garden,
rich and purple. And a single jay
visited, just once. But the magpies here
have got so bold they come right down in pairs
and flounce about on the lawn. That crafty squirrel
has another trick for getting at the birdseed,
and there's a new fox seems to have moved in,
suns himself on the grass or on the toolshed,
thinks he owns the place.

But all this will be nothing to you now,
and the spring, indifferent, has gone on without you.

Poetry He Said

Poetry he said will not
particularise; you ought to (seriously)
work at it.

We took our drinks up
and sat in a window looking over
the muddy river.

Poetry would not name
the pub or the place or the river,
but the muddy sky showed

it was not Eden
where we sat together. I thought of cockles,
their bleak windowless

lives and how they
would have no names for pub or river
or for happiness.

Another Autumn

Never a word to say what has become of him.
Last we heard he was heading for the Aegean
with a folder of lecture notes and a rolled-up beach towel,
bringing to young Constantine, Electra, Hector
the consolations of Lowell and Wallace Stevens.

Meanwhile in deltoid Britain with its doomed look
another autumn fades. They have polled the plane trees
in leafy Greenwich - they never cut so deep
until this year - and loaded the waving branches
on lorries, not a leaf or a stalk left lying
to clog the gutters. Made a neat job of it.

The birds were struck dumb. What will become of spring?
Will it ever come back? The stiff divested columns
stand idle in the streets like Trojan women
in the last act, but under a grey sky.

Gifts From The Garden

I send you, my dear, a wisp of cloud
caught in the crown of the flowering cherry,
a splash of ink from the smart blackbird's
intricate song he sings from the chimney.

I send you the sappy sigh of grass
in the whirr of the blades that graze it over,
a rattle or two of the magpie's laugh,
a ruffle of breeze from the cool magnolia,

a flick of the slick staccato squirrel,
a flash of blue from a jay's wing,
from the iceberg roses a breath, a shimmer,
and you are in England once again.

And summer's come, and perhaps you're sated
with wondering just what everyone's at
in a world where everything needs translating
and the signs are a puzzle on every street.

And it's good, for the moment, that you're back,
and the taste of the mother-tongue is sweet
like taking an old pipe down from the rack
(though the right-hand turn's a forgotten knack
and you're humming the tunes of distant places).

Rainy Day In The Strand

The gutters sob, this sky's like a wet sack,
everything squelches. Fat umbrellas flail,
shouldering the crowds to force a streaming passage.
No-one looks up. Colour drains from the day.
Rain on the hills was green. What has possessed me
to settle in this grey metropolis?

I try to picture clear Italian fields
and you mixing the ochres on your palette,
expert, observant, capturing the sunlight,
while here we shudder, watching the sun go backwards:
less light each day, more dampness. This today's
the very air and image of your absence -
streets and no trees, and everywhere the rain.

Sunday Afternoon Walk

The wall went up so high above the traffic,
above the heads, above the reach of everything,
on top was perfect safety - once you landed.
But the sparrow kept flying low, hovering, swooping
upwards; then the one on the ground would flutter
upwards, but always fell back on the pavement.
Two friends stopped in their walk and saw it all,
keeping their distance, willing the patient stratagem
of friendship to succeed, to inspire perhaps
at least the strength to flutter on to a ledge
low on the wall, away from clumsy feet.

The feet came on. Then the bird did not move.
It lay with beak opening, shutting on nothing.
Finished, I said. But she stooped with cupped hands
cradling the smashed wing, the disabled head,
knowing well such birds as this nothing can save,
no miracle. Still, wanting the miracle.
Too late. She laid it on a ledge in the wall,
and there we left it, and the living bird
high on the wall, that had seen everything
and had stopped swooping. And came home to tea.

"Woman Reading"

The light just touches hair and nape, gilds leaves
of the book beside her she bends to, turning away,
hunching a thin shoulder. She's wearing nothing,
but the glints and shadows clothe her as if they loved her.

The hand, you find, is not right - too flat to the body.
She will sit unmoving, giving herself to the book
while you squeeze and mix and whatever it is you do
to let in a little space under the knuckles,
taking your time, assessing the colour of shadow,
the precise angle of advancing daylight.

Later I come back and admire the magic
that has made a woman out of splashes of light
and shown her pondering over her book with patience
that's set in paint and will be infinite.
And I think of other moments in infinity
when dark shapes hovered over the landscape,
and how you used the skills that were always yours
brushing out unwanted shadows, letting in light.

End of the Line

In here is a very young woman
wondering what life will bring,
but tonight I am playing an old woman
all wrinkled and doddering.

And I have a stick and a bus pass
and a hood to keep off the rain,
and people are kind at bus stops
and give me their seat on the train.

But no-one knows where I've come from
so far along the track.
It's late and the gates are closing,
and now I can never get back.

Series Discontinued

The Tor has kept its old place on the map:
climbing another day we should still find
quilted counties deep in unruffled air.
The dizzying quarry where the jackdaws wheeled
with harsh plummeting cries must be still there.
And ordinary instruments would point the way
to giant-haunted Cader that let fall on us
pompoms of snow playfully out of an innocent sky.

Stern pines guard their long gloomy avenues.
Their stiff platoons reprove the rioting bracken
where we came out on an edge of the Chase and saw
the deer rise silently, mysterious earth-gods,
crowned with branches, sculpting the deep horizon.
In Dovedale we crossed barefoot on the warm stone
and lay on a bank spangled with light high over
the shimmering water, very close to heaven.

Now others live in the house where one still morning
you piped Brandenburg wagging your head to the tune.
They walk on Sundays in the abandoned cutting
where thorns bowed over the path and grass sprang up
between the cobbles, and a flaming crown
offered itself and showed its name - coltsfoot.
Spring after spring, it must be, there is coltsfoot
on the track. But we, my dear, where have we gone?

The Headland

Even now on occasion, powdering the wrinkles,
I meet a look of hers caught in the glass.
We know, too, how to make each other laugh still,
though things to laugh at now will take more finding.

And today I walk into the ward where someone
coming to our assistance, or perhaps
a fellow-patient, will be bound to tell me
what's plain to everyone, we must be sisters.

We might have been carved from a single block
 on some grey headland where the waves all day
plunge and plash, and the unflagging gulls
patrol forever. Only now begin
rumours of something grinding, something rending,
waves washing further in, further in.

Sisters in a Wood

We meet in the corridor, almost mirror images,
white heads bent over sticks at identical angles.
It is just on one, the hour fixed for my visit,
and the day is fine for us to sit under the trees.

Both have lived a long while, have grown tired,
and you say it would be good to lie on the grass.
It would be good, but for such stiff old scarecrows
it seems too much of a venture. We find benches.
But soon I see you are too tired for benches.

And perhaps I should have let you have your grass.
The trees here spread their mansions in the sky,
all quick with birds. And some of these, it may be,
would come and do what birds did in the old stories.
Then here we might lie quiet on the earth
and never stir, and those good birds would come
and cover us with leaves. And leaves. And leaves.

Ice

The sun climbs through the window, strokes your cheek.
Hour after hour you don't move from your chair,
hoping no-one will notice you in there,
no-one will touch your hand, no-one will speak.
Though you shun visits, saying you're too antique,
I've come. And you, long icebound in despair,
dredge up a smile at such sisterly care,
but the ice grips us, and our smiles are weak.
Life is the grief that throbs deep in the bone.
You long for wings, a sail, any device
to glide out of this world and this world's air,
then say you only want to see what's there.
What would you look for, voyaging alone
beyond the stars, through world on world of ice?

No Transmission

The lines are down. Still I spell out my message,
knowing the words won't break through in spring, in summer,
in a millennium. You longed for quiet,
and quiet came duly - Himalayas of quiet.

Drab days. The trees grow spectral. A few late roses
are moulting over the path. I'll miss our teatimes,
that narrow room where we'd still laugh together
over old times no-one else now remembers.

I'll miss telling you things. You'd smile at this one.
That plot at Kew beside the lily pond
you loved to haunt - that's where your impudent
ashes have come to rest. Don't ask who planted them.

You have the pick of shrubs for bedfellows,
they'll own your tribute every season now,
and as the year rolls round through spring, through summer,
you'll rise with the roses. I thought you'd like to know.

The Old Man Comes For Christmas

The kids have done with Christmas. Back to the box
that spills its routine magic. A room's focus
was once the blaze in the grate. Somewhere there's laughter.
I twist round in my chair, straining to listen,
feel for my pipe and pouch - and then remember.
I go to find my muffler, get some air,
but the girl hears me, runs out of the kitchen,
tells me this freezing snow is treacherous.

The unwrapped presents languish on the carpet.
There's a dog when you wind it wags its tail,
says *Woof!* An airport - all the floors light up,
the lifts work, and the signals. The bar has bottles.
I doze, and other winters come to mind,
lulled by the labials of dancing flames,
the luxury of walnuts, sips of wine,
songs about love, those wheezy old recordings
that whirled on the great wind-up gramophone
we'd dance to once, before the children came.

Where she is now the snow falls without hurt.

Trafalgar Ward, Greenwich D.H.

The man next the window
glares. He has Parkinson's.
Long before visiting's over he's on at the nurses
to draw the curtains and pack him into his bed.

The other side of me
there's one hitched night and day to this great machine
with a bellows in it. When he falls asleep
there's a sound of air sucked.

Visitors are scarce here,
talk mostly to each other. My daughter, though,
comes every day. Some days the words I want
won't come, or I can't tell what words I want.

We sit, waiting.
Later she'll take my pyjamas, go back to the cat.
Sometimes I feel him climbing
into my chair; then the dream goes.

Stray wisps of talk
drift in among the dreams. "Yes, ninety this year -
in December." Down in the park
the old year's leaves are getting ready to fall.

And there's a pigeon
I can see perched on the rail outside the window.
They say she has young there, huddled out on the ledge.
Their feathers are dark, they'll fly soon.

There's a new man
in the bed opposite. The light is going.
No more visitors now.
Soon they'll be round with the trolley.

An Inhospitable Place

Best have some sort of ID always ready
so they'll know you're on a visit, not an inmate,
and the doors will open when it's time to go.
Doors beyond doors. Locked. Unlocked. Locked again.

Pluto's hall not more cheerless. Vacant faces,
slackjawed, marooned in tall chairs spaced far out;
nothing to read, or do, no-one to talk to.
Beds ranged along a corridor, out of bounds.

Scanning physiognomies, we make out a shape
that should be hers. The stretched blue cardigan
must have been someone's, once. Nothing she's wearing
seems hers, none of it fits. The enshrouding cobwebs

drift. Will she know us still? In a stab of clarity
she implores us, *Don't remember me like this.*
Then an urgent, *keep this, please, for me.* Hands cupped,
close, round some memory no-one now can share.

Outside, the trees still ply their occupations,
the grass gets grassier, the wild things grow,
the air is sweet with birds. There are the buses
heading in all directions, free to go.

The Possessor of a Toothpick

There'd been an announcement that would rouse the dead
if any had been commuting. It roused the deaf
(whose aids exacerbate noise) raising the question
what was all that about? And now they want us
to report any *other technicalities.*
Or could that be *unattended packages*?
Travel's dicey when your hearing lets you down.

My TV offers subtitles (quaintly spelt);
radio's risky. *His first maid was thrown
in his garden* should be *his first maize was grown.*
A *fictional* girl mauled by a dog had been
a six-year-old. The possessor of a toothpick
turned out to be *a professor of acoustics.*
The government, I hear, has shot seven people.
Good heavens! Whose government? Oh it was a *gunman.*
When the wild boar made changes in a woman,
it had been a *woodland* that the wild boar changed.

Working this out takes time. Fast speech is missed speech.
So's any speech struggling with competition,
parties, large gatherings. No wonder if
the deaf scuttle off home, private as beetles
not wanting to bother anyone, or themselves.
We still have quiet talks in quiet rooms
with a few friends. And books. And there's the garden.
When leaves rustle or bees sing on their rounds
their syllables need no interpreting.
I never have to grovel and tilt my ear
with *Sorry, I missed all that. What's that you were saying
after "Something amazing happened on Wednesday morning"?*

The Ever Gracious Minister

"Been good to torture you," says the interviewer.
"Good to be tortured" would seem the apt reply.
I could be wrong of course. When your hearing goes
vowels just leave you groping. The series of telephones
that exploded the other day were *terrorist bombs*.
And the ever gracious minister was the one
concerned with *immigrations*. Then odd accents
can scupper sense. The problems with her diamonds
the east-ender said his wife had were with *ailments*.
And Americans who call for a cannibal government
just want an *accountable* one. And here we have
a rum non sequitur: "He burnt his coffee
and bought a caravan." Could it be he *let his cottage*?
It's an eerie world. Didn't you say this winter
each time the door was opened a free giraffe
ran through the house? I could be wrong of course.

Going To The Polls

"Saw's a killer!" she says as we pass on the street.
I signal my sympathy, wondering as usual
what I've agreed to this time. Sun, wind, cold -
nothing seems in excess. But this is polling day.
Could it be, possibly, something political?
I was a fervent voter once. Now only
long habit and the Pankhursts keep me going.
This time, whoever wins, expect disaster.
Toiling on up the hill, I solve a mystery:
What she said must have been, "This hill's a killer."

Talking of Travel

Great to be back, they say, stuffing the washing-machine
and telling you how they nearly didn't make it,
how the cable failed in the Tunnel, leaving the ferry
to dawdle across and dump them by night in Dover,
or how they dossed down at the airport, or howled with rage
as their luggage careered ahead on a different journey.
Never again, they say. Wonderful to be home.

But the next plane that goes zooming across the sky
crammed with expectant tourists, each compressed
like something a canning factory might have processed,
puts them in mind they could be zooming too.
Because how else are they going to hold their own
when they face the question where did you go this year,
if they didn't get to gawp at the Taj Mahal
or join the queues at the Louvre, see the Winged Victory,
or cross St Mark's Square dodging turbulent pigeons?

These days when everyone shuffles in line at Heathrow
you quickly understand you are no-one at all
if you only went to Brighton, and less than no-one
if you sat in your garden as long as the sun was out
enjoying the shade of your trees and the butterfly dances,
and when the sun went in, went in to your books;
and the sights you went to see were in galleries
by the dear old Thames, where tourists flock each summer.

And soon there'll be the new brochures. What do you say to
the Rhineland this year for a change, or doing the Nile?
We must find out the jabs we need and about the insurance.
And who will look after the cat? Here I slip away
to spare them my dereliction of convention.
I'll be hearing the bees sing loud in the lavender
or scribbling a line of verse if the verse is willing,
or stuck with my nose in a book or walking to shops,
greeting again and again the same old neighbours
in genial Charlton, tucked in leafy Greenwich.

Tracking Down 4B

Our first day back, I'm starting with 4B
but find I don't know what room they'll be in
or where the books are I must take with me.

I ask, but it seems no-one gives a pin.
I tour the classrooms to suss out a space
where a mob waits for action to begin.

They could be watching, jeering, as I pace
all round the quad, pausing at every door.
Or could it be I've come to the wrong place?

I can't remember cloisters here before
or anywhere I've taught, in all my days,
or that long featureless dim corridor

where something's stirring in the paint's dark glaze.
There's someone there - this can't be a mistake -
who gazes out at me just as I gaze,

trying to get things clear, till my eyes ache:
a haggard form, ravaged beyond repair,
growling, "You old buffoon, why don't you wake?

It's twenty years since you taught anywhere."

Voyage of Discovery

I wanted to be a writer of bestsellers,
a glamorous filmstar or perhaps a queen,
so they wouldn't be always tugging at my tangles
and saying how grumpy and untidy I'd been.

Only work hard was what they always told me,
you'll be surprised to find what you can do.
Success was waiting round the corner for me.
I dared not say I hoped romance was too.

People in books lived happy ever after;
somewhere out there must be true happiness.
And sages held out promise of nirvana
to staunch and focussed seekers after bliss.

Voyaging through time I had to take some sail in;
the scope must wane as the lifeblood grows cool.
Out there beyond the horizon el dorado
gleamed more phantasmal, less accessible.

It's been a long run. A descending silence
whispers I'm somewhere near the end of it.
And happiness? There's harbouring for a quiet
acknowledgement of things being adequate.

Unremarkable Day

I thank you God (in case you should happen to be there -
well, who can be sure?) for this most remarkably
unremarkable day. I get to the shops still,
and there's a bus I will clamber on gingerly.

I've had some falls but nothing was really broken,
and neighbours hurried to bounce me back on my feet.
There's water still in the taps though the drought goes on,
and a cosy chair where I love to read or sleep.

I lunch in the garden where butterflies dance - a few of them -
and a squirrel almost ventures to drink at the water bowl
set there for marauding casuals, types like him.
But he can't quite trust me. Some other time he'll call.

Later I'll get my stick and go shambling off to visit
the friend who mellows and moulders along with me.
Our scope's not great but the talking and tea are pleasant.
L'enfer c'est les autres? Non moins le paradis.

A Celebration: for A.J.

Our eighty-something summers
afford this little space
to rest and look about us
and gape at the universe.

A fly alights on the page
just half a comma high
then, adept in aeronautics,
takes off along the sky.

And the plants here are so learned
if they can't hear or see
they bring themselves to perfection
with no hint from anybody,

while the young, risen out of darkness,
impetuous and frail,
stride out against the universe
not doubting they are able.

But craggy dinosaurs trapped
in a slick digital age
can only shudder and fumble
at an alien heritage,

and would lose heart perhaps
but, life's dear miracle,
this earth that formed and frames you
can be a kind earth still.

THREE BIRTHDAY POEMS

For Audrey in May

Glad of the sunshine, I'd welcome a May month that went on
all the year long, the warmth on my shoulder as tender
as touch of a friend, the dearest. There'd always be riots of roses
and the sun would be dancing and clapping hands over and over,
happy to find us together.

A time of thanksgiving. Though Darwin has scuppered the myth
  of Creation,
this day is a blessing: I'm half on my knees adulating
whoever might still be Out There, though the shrines are all empty
  and undone,
while I bask (still suspecting I owe a burnt offering to someone)
in your ninetieth, glad of the sunshine.

Birthday Poem for Audrey

Here's one more year we've scored, snatched from the dark,
and summer's back with bumblebees and roses,
though in these dithery days what no-one knows is
how long our iPads can be got to work.
But let's jog on together hoping we're
good for another and another year.

Most of All
Our last birthday poem

Most of all you - with sable brush to capture
flushed petals, twigs hastily burgeoning,
the season's enterprise, the thrushes' rapture -
can teach a simple sketchpad how to sing.

And I, trailing long chains of years behind me,
am glad to have another springtime here,
glad of the twittering trees, the sap that's rising,
the sunshine when there's sunshine and, my dear,
most of all you.

GREEN AND PLEASANT LAND

A Home

People retire to the country; I do it the wrong way round.
Sick for the ditch-lined roads, the rookeries,
the streams winding through woods, the fields, the spaces,
I choose to settle in this grey metropolis
for friendship's sake, to be in the same town.

So we go to look at houses. This one won't do,
pebbledashed, dark inside, all blacks and browns.
Hard to imagine it cheerful. Best be going.
Then they show us the garden - shrubs and shady trees
stretching away to where a magnolia spans
greenhouse and shed; beyond that, rising ground,
a steep bank with more trees, a tangled waste
where no-one comes. There's quiet here, and greenness.
You could sit beneath the magnolia and breathe,
and never know it's London. And the house?
Well, there's paint, isn't there? So now I live here.

I've rural neighbours. Foxes ravage the borders,
leave relics of their partying, bones, old shoes.
Their young romp on the lawn before the sun's up.
And once I watched a mouse hoarding the birdseed
that fell from a feeder. Every feeder I had
squirrels have broken up. One of them once
would take nuts from my hand. This generation
keep their distance, flickering along the branches.
Up there the magpies rattle and scold and brawl,
then pace the lawn ceremonious as nabobs.

In summer dandelions leap from cracks in the paving,
daisies dance on the grass; holly and elder
wrestle lovingly, and an anarchic bramble
leans out from the rhododendron offering blackberries.
Frogs live in the undergrowth; sometimes at twilight
one will flop indiscreetly out of the ivy.
And Mabel (that's the name on the medal she wears)
of no known address, purrs on the bench beside us,
ecstatic, when we take our tea on the patio.
Home is for this, a place to be happy in.

Encounter

A sharp young face outside the patio door
interrogates the room. I freeze and watch,
and wonder how things seem to an interloper
come slinking through the trees and tangled scrub
beyond the wall, that waste ground colonised
by disinherited foxes.

And how, in spite of fences, spite of boulders
dragged in to shore up weak points where the ground gives,
he and his kind come romping over the borders,
dismantling reckless pigeons on the lawn,
wrestling and chasing as if they owned the place still,
sampling the night life.

Still, wildlife must be cherished. The fox my brother.
Well, cousin, say. A matter of genes between us,
some measly percentage, science would have the number.
He's no reader though, does his own experiments,
finds (having put the matter to the test)
all that's between us glass.

New Neighbour

I hadn't lived here long and was coming home,
treading deserted pavements lined with cars
all drawn up neatly, waiting for the morning,
when something crossed the road beyond the lamplight.
Not quite a cat. Less fluid, more elongated.
A fox! On a street here, at night, in London?
I stood and watched, wondering where he'd go now
between the close-ranked houses. Where could he go?
He didn't. He stood rooted to the pavement
and watched me watching him across the street.
Stalemate. Neither would move. I gave in first,
and as I moved he moved too, slinking off
behind the cars. I never saw where he went.
But why he stopped has sometimes set me wondering.
If this was his beat could he have been surprised
at one more of us humans returning home
at the sort of hour when humans do return,
or simply wondering at my surprise?

To a Blue Butterfly

You have known death of a sort and a strange madness,
to frowst in a narrow room, at last break out
finding you've been morphed into someone else,
someone the air belongs to, and the summer.
And the past could be another universe
or a fiction, something Borges might have dreamt up.

Our own past stalks us like an indignant spectre;
the future lures and daunts, whetting its jaws.
But the butterfly world's a world untroubled by tenses:
the future is someone else's, the past no more
than a cast-off chrysalis, nothing in there to bother
you laughing at fences, flitting free as a zephyr,
alighting, retiring, inscrutable dancer, advancing
from light into light with never a thought of tomorrow.

Frog In Ivy

So it's you again, little frog, catapulting on to the paving
as I tear despondently at the tangled ivy,
trying to clear a bed. I startle mildly
in this half-light. Can't quite see who you are.

An error of judgement launched you on to my path -
which we try to retrieve by pretending it never happened,
till you have made it safely across the border
where you sit in the dark, I imagine, glad of your luck.

And I'm glad of this brief acquaintance I've struck up
with one who won't call me a clumsy gardener
or complain that I'm absent-minded and slow-witted.
That may well be, as humans go, the kind you prefer.

For to you we must seem like gods, serene, prodigious,
with nothing to fear from any creature on earth.
Oh, little frog, if you knew how some of us humans
will skulk in the ivy just for a bitter word!

Jays on the Lawn

For a Silver Wedding

Today when the whole sky rattled and shook with a demon cackle
and the treetops quaked till a gaggle of birds bounced out of them,
and cats lost their siesta,

somebody said, "It's those jays!" But jays - well, take a look at them
out on the lawn there, so quiet. You hardly ever see one
but when you look round there's the other

dawdling some way up the garden, inspecting the lawn and the border,
just as the first one you saw is inspecting the lawn and the border.
You'd think they were quite unconnected,

barely on speaking terms, as they settle to their prospecting,
not keeping an eye on the other, but always uncannily managing
never to widen the distance

too much. It's as if a current hummed through the field between them,
informing, protecting, sustaining, how can we know what it's doing -
some force almost palpably there.

Just so it must sometimes be in the vintage years of a marriage -
though scuffles among the foliage will alarm the serenest of gardens,
and even in Eden (I'm guessing)

feathers must sometimes be ruffled, sometimes the rain must fall,
berries can't be at their juiciest all the year round, it takes ripeness -
here out of time's distillations

something is centering down to depths far out of the storms' reach,
where currents subtler than water, air, thought even, were always
feeding a lily-pond stillness.

Spring In The City

Our London spring these days begins in winter.
The magnolia that straddles half the garden
can't wait till February to bring its buds out.
They'll grow to giant blooms before the leaves come,
need a prompt start. Then suddenly you'll see
a chorus of crocuses flaunting their purple.
They've been invisible, clenched against the cold.

And now platoons of stiff municipal tulips
stand to attention all day in the park,
and supermarkets sell for ninetynine pence
sad-looking sheaves that when you get them home
explode next day into the sort of trumpets
that would leave Wordsworth gasping. It's spring all right.

The birds wake early, they can't wait for daylight
to whistle up the morning. Trees go green now.
That's when the heart lifts. Then diminutive daisies
and buttercups in troupes slyly invade
what's meant to be my lawn. If mowing bans them,
in two or three days they'll be back for sure,
dauntless and dancing. Their coming half consoles me
for fields and lanes I used to wander in,
with tremulous flora peeping from the hedgerows
and woods that nurtured cool dark violets
when lark and cuckoo claimed the world for theirs.

In a Summer Garden

Here is a space for quiet, here where the gradual ferns
are closing in on the bench where you sit so still
the blackbird drinks from the basin at your elbow,
a wasp will sip from the brink and sense no peril.

This is not *your* garden you've cultivated here:
on the lawn the jay is prospecting; a squirrel swings
on the bird-feeder the bluetits thought was theirs,
and this is the corner where a fat spider spins.

You've barely opened your book when right on the table
a fly alights and broods on its dark reflection,
and a bold blue butterfly dances over the ivy
where a blue butterfly's the crown of creation.

So you muse or drowse until the expostulating
magpie's rattle shatters the dream and the glamour.
Shrivelled and dizzy from orbiting round the sun,
here you do nothing but merge in a murmur of summer.

In Praise Of Summer

Spring, yes - the quickening shiver in the wind
turning to fitful mildness, a dawn shrillness
under the eaves, season of green prospects -
always the poet's darling.

                         Or gusty autumn
gauded with berries, the yellow deaths of leaves,
the year going up in bonfires, turning away from the sun,
the flickering swallows deserting.

                         Then the clear melancholy
of stripped winter, whimper of winds in the chimney,
deep journey into the dark; or under a flannel sky
miraculous dazzle of snow.

                         And all of these
have songs: our desks are stuffed with poems to them
chanting their procession toward or from the light
that lengthens into summer -

                         that scattered dozen
of days warm enough for sitting out in the garden -
most evanescent of seasons, our pick of the year.
But who writes odes to summer?

                         Dear languid days,
haunt of the lark and cuckoo, when bees go bumbling
and roses pout and blouse, and we unbutton,
breathe, almost become, the sun.

                         How can we sing them?
Like happy marriages, they leave us dumb.

Under The Leaves

Lying out under the leaves,
the wind's tide in the trees
saying all that's left to be said
of summer and the end of summer,

or seeing the rooks row home
with the best of the light gone,
black wings, cumbersome, spread
in a requiem of colour,

and the bench where we drank tea
nudged by the unmannerly
magnolia no-one pruned
disappearing into the shade,

I hear in the wind's whispers
rumours beyond existence
that float like a vanished music
and fade as the leaves fade.

Islands

What is it about islands sets us all clamouring,
"That's for me"? Is it the palm fronds
that wave in the breezes, the washed beaches,
the untouched springs that so long awaited
our great arrival? Is it the thatched hut,
simple but adequate, built by our own hands,
curtained with creepers, the abundance of wild herbs
we'd always instinctively know how to use?

Or just not having to mow the lawn, iron shirts
or arrange about the insurance. And being able
to get to grips at last with Shakespeare and the Bible
or Bhagavad-Gita perhaps, and in the long nights
really study the stars and not have to listen
to anyone snoring, since we know we'd be
there all alone. How else could we learn to savour
the desolation of gulls and the desert within
that we always meant, someday, to visit seriously,

where, long before we grew obsessed with the need
to change our library books or look for a dentist,
or that snap of the Venice tour got curled at the edges
or eaten by ants, and the diet of bananas and coconuts
palled, we'd concede the always turning wheel,
castaways from birth, each on a narrow island
in the sighing of tides bemoaning a lost mainland
where we could be chatting, serene on a well-kept lawn,
pleased with the chink of teacups, idling and dreaming of islands.

A Horticultural Question

The horticulturists were in a ferment.
Someone had asked, "Which flower is most like love?"
Some said a red red rose and some a hyacinth
with all the merry bells it's made up of.
Others would give the title to the lilies
because they toil not, neither do they spin.
The sundew was the favourite of the cynics:
it sucks your blood fast as it draws you in.
Some opted for the daffodil's brazen trumpet
that calls to arms and stirs the blood of youth,
and some the dandelion because the poet
has written, "Love is like the lion's tooth."
Ah, but the SNOWDROP comes with earth's great freeze on,
nods, and at once proclaims a change of season.

Autumn Takes Over

This time of year when I go down to check
on the cypress I planted it's hard to escape arrest
from floating filaments spun out so rare
I'm always surprised by their groping who-goes-there.

"The owner, that's who." But is that quite the tone?
Who can ever feel, "This garden is all my own"?
Not the squirrel whose larder it is, the jays that farm it,
nor the careful fox who nightly inspects and marks it.

And not this bumbling biped who oils the gear
and locks it away and may not be seen there all winter,
or ever, while buds go on growing and bulbs for the spring,
and the garden smiles in secret and manages everything.

It's cold. I go in to write while the leaves turn,
the hollies burnish their berries, the mists come on,
and I try for words that will sing as the light ebbs,
but it's dark in my head, a season of cobwebs.

Winter Coming

This is the place, though you will not come now,
where summer beckoned bold in blandishment
and the untamed magnolia bough on bough
whirling like Shiva spread its dappled tent.
But winter glowers. The spruce blackbird waits,
weighing his chances while I rake the leaves;
the squirrel at the back door contemplates
the proffered nut one daring move retrieves.
Earth's dank now, grey. Mad winds are muttering
spells to confound before they come to pass
the insidious machinations of the spring -
the greens, the golds, the laughter in the grass
that will dispute what they can't quite deny,
that each new autumn is a new goodbye.

Robin and Rake

Dull day in the garden,
dank, and the sky dank,
and all these leaves to be cleared.

A flickering in the air
(fluff? feathers? a puff of breath?)
troubles my sightline.

Barely an arm's length distant,
there on the ground. No, there.
Next moment, up on a bough

briefly. Now at my feet,
back turned, half trustingly,
pausing to reconnoitre.

Then in a flick he's gone.
Well, it's the leaves I'm here for,
my rake goes swishing through.

And abracadabra he's back,
alert head, breast aglow,
sitting for his picture.

Most birds stay aloof. Not robins.
Twitchers, they always find
something to watch in humans.

Zero

This feather-footed snow
arrives so slyly
the world's entirely
turned topsy-turvy
before you know.
The sky's clay-coloured,
brooding and surly.
Windows are eerily
lit from below.

Gulls driven inland
circle the houses;
their resolute wings shear
the blanket of air;
but trying for foothold
they shudder and founder,
missing known passageways,
tossed among silences,
trespassers there.

The mind too circles,
disconsolate, weightless,
sensing its strangeness
in alien air
in a blank season
between old spent roses
and the new sleek crocus,
transient in transience,
nesting nowhere.

In Time Of Elm Sickness

Along the path to the wood they are felling the broad
sinewy elms. Unsafe: a sickness insidiously
gnawing within is crumbling trunk and limb.
Here you see in the sawn ends the tawny
dark-fretted wound hollowing the pale strength.
Sinuously insistent, seeking out depth and length,
how the midget army through branch and bole bit!

Day-long the thin high vibrant whine
of the lithe power-saw hones the keen wind.
Pyres flare night-long devouring infected timber.
They call to mind what I too well remember:
the long nights flaring on another hill
in the plague year with death-fires of cattle.
No passing-bells for elms that die like this.

Not all must perish, levelled to a smooth plinth.
Some have kept their heads, and some still
stand, lifting lopped limbs to the glancing wind,
strong to withstand a whisper-soft seeping
at the still root, and in air, resistless,
where ruin's final, to court the casual
innuendoes of birds settling in unmaimed trees.

Betrayed to corruption, still they stand, sketching
the delicate fan-line, controlled rapture
of those whose age will be graceful and vigorous,
the elm-gesture - but truncated,
leper-stumps lifted not in prayer but
deprecation: "Remember, remember,
I Fradubio was once an elm like you."

Owls

The first night of my death let owls be heard
quartering the woods, and let a tall angel
reach me a long ear-trumpet to catch the words
of their eerie dialogue. Then after ages
wedged in with London's traffic I'll take flight
above the streets and grave meridional Greenwich
and the dapper memorial lawns of Golders Green
and finally know where I am and what has happened,
that woods have owls still and everything's all right.

The Touch of Earth

Antaeus son of Earth, both feet on the ground
or one foot only, was indomitable.
Earth fed him strength through touch: Hercules found
lifting him clear the only way to kill.
Our life's in cities. Earth's a poor alien
prisoned under paving, dispossessed foxes trail
from street to street, the sparrows are all gone
from a world never dark and never still -
far cry from his who lived when there were gods
in forest and furrow, and could stay his needs
on herbs and curds and berries, his roof's low beams
fragrant with woodsmoke where the shadows breathed
mimicking the firelight, and the owls' tremulous hoots
echoed for miles above the unmanaged woods.

Water in its Phases

There was a beck ran down beside the cottage
and frisked about and rollicked over boulders
and sang all through the night in varying voices
that broke in on the soundtrack of our dreams.

Ovid no doubt would name the nymph that played there
and yarn about some swain coming with tribute
when revellers would linger in the half-light
to see her spread her hair out on the foam.

But Ovid's nymphs are put to flight by neon -
a lightness goes when light is all-pervading -
water is tamed in ways that would amaze him,
and tribute's paid now to the Water Board.

It's a commodity like any other
though the books tell and we sometimes remember
it was the mother of life from the beginning
and what it gave can any time recall.

The Sea

You'd never guess, seeing the dangerous glint
in the eye she turns to the stars - to the sun, even -
this was the mother of mothers. Was the first flutter
of life cherished and bred in her cold fluids?

Estranged now since our ancestors emigrated
trusting to dry land, she will suffocate us
given half a chance. When we venture on her domain,
taking all due precautions, she can still get at us.

We in our turn abduct her citizens
in shoals, and infest her with our toxic leavings
till she'll swell and rise and engulf the lot of us,
and the glint in her eye will be what it always was.

Into the Depths

The seagulls wheel and scream and dive for their dinner;
whales saunter by, singing to one another.

Round warmer waters patient corals labour;
in their intricate cities everything happens in colour.

Descend. Here the sun's beams will never come;
undulant spectral dances haunt the gloom,

strange orifices gape and nameless lives
dimly pulsate, no need to open your eyes.

Then down, down where the sea's weight lies heavy
on the encrusted wrecks of some spoiled navy,

leave light and life and everything behind you.
Down there, silence and silt. No-one will find you.

Grass

All spring the grass ran riot; the hedge billowed
nudging aside the path; insidious ivy
writhing from tree to tree was fettering everything
that didn't know how to run or where to shelter.

There's been a change. Here as we sit in the sun
the wild herbs keep their heads below the paving;
the lawn is sleek - cared for, neighbours would say.
(Grass goes its way, not likely to be grateful.)

Wilderness dwindles, wayside flowers are going,
bees work less and less at their heady ferment.
A fox rears up to peer through the patio window,
baffled by glass, uncertain where his world went.

What will inherit Earth after the last
green field crumbles, last city lies flat?
Silence. And death. But, should the least rift come
in the grudging rubble, would the grass tiptoe back?

A Tree

A pointless puzzler: if you were to choose
a tree your bones would feed when you were dead,
which would it be? I thought of whispering poplars
that bless our cramped suburbs. I thought of elms
casting their dark nets into the sky, circled
by scolding rooks that let the townsman know
he's made it to the border; green-pillared beeches
spreading a vaulted shade; rough oaks, hospitable
to owls and squirrels, living almost forever,
offering meals in cups; then delicate birches
that shimmer in woods and beckon or surprise
like half-hidden laughter. All these could have my bones
and welcome.
                But once in a corner of a field,
bent by the wind, its roots clutching the hillside,
with twisted sinews, tiny resistant leaves,
one hawthorn braved the skyline where we rested
that day, faint from walking. When woods are dying,
in that last long-foretold calamity,
when no-one's left on earth, not even a fieldmouse,
and dust muffles the silence, there could be one tree
with shrubby insistence clutching a crumbling world,
only a little longer. And it might be
in that outpost of time your ghost would come
to mourn the trees and walk where it was green once,
tracking the desolation mile on mile,
thirsting for wildness and the curlew's call,
and find my tree, and rest there for a while.

Climbing Cader Idris

A fierce front you turned to us, Cader Idris,
ice-cold encouragement,
frowning darkness in your gnarled rock.
A crisp wind pinned us to the cracking north face,
pounding to numbness; bucking boulders threw us;
struggling upright we met the lash of hail.
So, in the teeth of everything - or almost everything:
for, once, you did relent, proffering a moment
(like a wry sudden smile or a mild remark)
the almost forgotten homeliness of grass
and level walking before the last rough haul -
we gained the summit, that clutter of tragic rock,
and saw where the giant struck
his thinker's pose through all those shivering winters.

We could see everything, right to the world's edge -
if it was the world we were still standing on,
those yellow uninhabited undulations
insubstantial-seeming as a sunset sky.
Suppose some sly
trickster had whisked the world from under our feet
and no way down? I had to look and see.

Finally, eschewing boulders and the north wind,
we creep down by a steeper pathway,
steps cut in the rock and icicles glazing the face of it,
till we come to a winding shute old-timers know
by the name of the Fox's Path; down we go
in a flurry of soil erosion. And so, old Cader,
you kicked us out, and a good round dozen or two
armfuls of shale in the bargain - a gentle riddance
and quicker, no doubt, than coming down a ladder.

At the foot I look back, reading in that timeless frown
a rich malice, impersonal.
Not again, never lightly, would I scale
that stiff ungenial flank, that stony shoulder.
And yet, days later,
leaving Wales, passing just that pattern of grey boulder,
I start at a strange quickening, feel it move,
this germ of a birth in me that shoots like love.

SOME PORTRAITS

Which Portrait Painter?

If it's noblesse you're after, Titian's your man,
his gods all grace, his humans so serene,
sublime, you may be sure, since time began,
nothing about them had been plain or mean.

Holbein's for people of consequence: his duchess,
almost a child still, yet had what it took
to resist a Tudor; his robed ambassadors
invite the death's-head's hollow, envious look.

The Dutch don't go for swank: a Rembrandt face
holds our straight gaze, not aiming to look handsome,
eloquent of life which, as the eyes confess,
they found no triumph and no martyrdom
but simply something we must all get through.
Here is your own self looking out at you.

Identities

You might think who you are's a simple question,
but things can quickly change, as Ovid knew.
Rest in a strange place, glance in a wrong direction,
you'd morph to bear, or stag, and no more you;

while, should you be inordinately clever,
outsmart the jealous gods, and get their goat,
you'd soon find you were worse off altogether
and end up as a spider or a stoat.

But some poor mortals driven to desperation
by cruelties of fate that made them fail
the gods could at their own sublime discretion
turn to a swallow or a nightingale.

It wouldn't mend their case to give them wings,
just change the perspective they must have on things.

A Question for Descartes

Descartes thought that, because he thought, he was.
Granted, he *thought* he was, and what that meant,
the solid sense, he need not doubt because
there were his books bolstering the argument,

his words, his name for all the world to see.
But if one day he did not know his name
and didn't even know the books that he
had written or the thoughts that were his fame,

or where he lived, or whether Truth was true,
could not find words, or tie his own cravat,
but groped through shifting shadows and never knew
just where he stood or what he would be at -

oh then, Descartes, what would you think or feel?
What if it's only love that makes us real?

George Claessen Nearing Ninety

Still working so late! There's a chill breeze, even angels
ought to be folding their wings and resting their halos.
But what's that to you, lost in voluptuous paint -

as you let yourself be lost, one time or another,
in a contemplation of rhino or elephant
that would set the image breathing within the frame.

Not just the line was right - the line was right -
but the animals came humbly, quietly,
and filled it with their presence and looked out on
the world they came from, not seeming to feel strange.

And there's something shares the secret of their quiet,
some wandering winding entity that dances
in slow mysterious ripple across a canvas,
serene and vivid as sunsets, uttering peace -

like that peace where we found you by the roadside,
having come by the wrong train. You had no paper
to pass the time, nor were you peering to see

if we were coming, but - pondering the mere routine
of traffic passing the point, much like that stream
Heraclitus saw, never two moments the same -

looked as if, had we not then chanced to see you,
you might have sat there twenty, thirty years
unshakeable, with that mild Buddha gaze.

Millbank Steps
i.m. John Robert Phillips

You took my hand. The steps went up and up.
Behind us lay a funny sort of seaside -
you said it was the Thames, a famous river.
There old Big Ben's lit face was, and the Tate
with rooms so high and echoey and huge
it made us walk on tiptoe, talk in whispers.

I wondered at all the poised, painted people.
Their stories flowed about them - steel Cophetua
subdued beneath his throne, softly admiring
the barefoot girl; Chaucer reading his Tales;
mad open-eyed inert Ophelia
and the shadowy lady in our Tennyson
buoyed on the mythic river; the boy Raleigh,
beached, with that blue gaze following the sailor's story,
seeing it all, impatient for his tide.

After the war the crowds began to arrive,
startled the echoes and unstrung the silence.
The pictures grew more tolerant and friendly;
who would have thought we'd share them with so many?
As years unrolled, nodding on a bench we'd find you.
Too stiff to tramp the boards adoring old loves,
you found it comforting to feel them round you.

And still the domes recall a small clenched man
who'd climb the steps half sideways in a shuffle,
clutching his stick, his face tense with the strain;
but when he'd got his breath back - oh, he'd smile then
like a schoolboy perched high among the apples.
I never saw a face transfigured quite
like his, some blank November afternoon
among his favourite Turners drenched in light.

Anniversary

He knew where all the small roads ran
where foot of man might go,
the cleanest way to leap a stream
or ford a shallow,

and the name of every bird
on twig or wing
that flaunted plumes to the wind
or sang in hiding.

The first faint cuckoo was his
and he would hear
the rusty cough of a pheasant
before another.

And the fluttering tip-tailed wren,
that puny challenger
armed with the staggering song,
could not fool his ear.

Born to observe and note,
to feel and know,
cherishing form and feature
in field and furrow,

if a stoat flickered over the road
or a squirrel out of a coppice
or chaffinches started a chase
he was first to notice.

He could whistle clear as a flute,
at peace, domestic,
waking a wandering ripple
of airy music,

or lift a verse from a page
to turn and show,
his cool voice holding it steady,
serene, mellow.

The paths are grown over now,
the streams run dry;
the flutes rehearse their wooden music
distantly.

The birds' songs are all blurred,
and what bent wing now
cleaves through the muted summer, neither
cuckoo nor crow?

Exit a Princess

You had it all, they said, allure, wit,
all the wealth in the world to go with it,
and - so the story went - lightness of heart.
We rustled our programmes, willing the play to start.

But waiting in the wings were the usual rout,
trolls, ogres, genies fizzing to get out,
the griefs, the ghosts wringing their saintly hands -
no expense spared, a cast of thousands.

Fumbling and stumbling - that's how most life is,
but royal stumbles are state circuses.
Tall shadows haunt the palace and the plot -
they get you in the end, princess or not.

In Aunt Mona's House

Aunt Mona was always one for a laugh -
hardly in through the door
before she'd set the whole room in a roar.
She'd fling her head back, and all that red hair
(she didn't believe in going grey, she said -
time enough for that after you were dead)
and laugh too till the gold fillings showed.

"You've quite made our day," we'd all say,
hustling her out on to the road
for the last bus. "Are you really sure you won't stay?"
But she'd have to go anyway
with that old grey parrot stuck in the house alone.

And then one rain-soaked day
there was only the parrot. A neighbour got the key,
and the chill closed in all round us.
It was getting too dark to see,
only there was this mirror twisted out of place,
and something shivered in it - a chalk-white face,
red-eyed, framed in a mass of hennaed hair.
It caught our gaze and vanished instantly.

Then that old parrot gave us all a scare,
crying in high sobs over and over - no making it
stop. "Archie! oh Archie!" we heard it call
in just Aunt Mona's voice - there was no mistaking it.
But "Archie"? Of course there never was an Archie.
Nobody'd ever heard of him at all.

Dialogue with Plum Tree

"That must come down," she says, "that old tree
stuck in the corner - see how its roots lift the paving."

(Those brash red bricks even the weeds cannot quell!)

I shift my gaze like a conspirator
where you lean twisting your roots at the narrow yard's end.
(Yes, and the cold shadowy damp that fosters
the green satanic mosses, horned ferns,
fronds that whisper slyly waiting the word to proliferate,
making the red one green - would any of this
be here if you were not?)

                "You must admit
it's no beauty," she says.

                My eye fondles
a stark gnarled limb groping across the wall
over the roof of the shed where starlings nest.
Between bouts of stuffing their clamorous young they rest
in your branches briefly. Cats climb, writhe,
angle for the fledglings safe under the roof.
In summer in a riot of leaves you will bring forth
a few flushed plums, wasps rolling in the pulpy sweetness,
dead drunk. And in barest winter there are always
boughs waving, wingbeats. When I stand at the kitchen window
we exchange smiles.

                "What's that you just said?"

He Comes Back

So he comes back, now the kids are grown and flown
and she's found her feet on the loner's slippery way,
got friends, work, things, a new life of her own,
no longer feels the scars or bemoans the day
he piled his bags in the hall and strapped them down,
then thanked her courteously and went his way.

He was always a charmer so now - broke, bent and frail,
finding his latest love wear rather thin -
once more goes buccaneering and sets sail
for an old haven that might serve again,
quipping *Love comes back to his vacant dwelling.*
She remembers the good times and takes him in.

Once in possession he gives no quarter. Soon
the house fills with his junk, then more arrives.
He takes his ease, while her work's never done.
New claims press in from old imprudences;
he smiles and pours more wine, preens, dreams in the sun.
His dreams expand; their funds never suffice.

You think you've heard it all before perhaps,
love festering in a knot there's no untying.
Man's a deceiver; speech was given for that,
and serves him well. Just think, if I'd been trying
to tell you a tiger, a boar, a bear came back
and moved right in, you'd know I must be lying.

Remembering B.W.

(03.06.15 - 20.09.05)

Because of the laughter that was in her voice,
when she told you her woes it was like sharing a feast.
Going through them could take whole evenings.

First were the trials of age: Methuselah,
she'd have you think, was her junior. Then the medics
lying in wait to get their hands on her; neighbours
always *popping in* to be sure she was all right;
and sly antique dealers - once over the threshold
their eyes were everywhere. And the racket next-door!
And the old good shops all finished, and television
going to the dogs: look at their Darcy - that
stuffed gorilla! So we'd chart the long decline,
connoisseurs of doom, pondering the mad career
of the world we saw ourselves as due to exit,
till the hand ached holding the handset.
Who now will talk to me about the old places?

October's not over, the sun not gone from the year,
and I sit in the garden alert to the whisper of leaves
as they fly on the wind that is hustling us into the dark.
She could have gone on for years savouring the banquet,
pronouncing on the cuisine. But the motor-cyclist
did not stop. Who knows if I'll miss her long?
One sip more of the blackbird's note and I too could be gone.

A Late Friendship

For Sylvia Naish, d. 21.02.96

Not family, picking my way among delicate questions,
I ask finally, is there any point in my staying?
They say you just might stir, are "very poorly".
(In their language all patients are "comfortable"
who are not dying.) I never knew this look,
swollen in angry sleep, clutching at breath.

I try to remember your keen delicate
crinkling-with-mischief face, the way you'd prompt me
in the back of the Russian class with words I needed
and made me keep on coming long after I knew
I'd started the classes too late. And that raw morning
in Harley Street, sharp with the dread of all
you might be told - sunk in the waiting-room chairs,
helpless as upturned beetles - still we found ways
to make each other smile. But when I rang
far into winter when pain had shrilled to madness -
could I do anything? - then, with that old wry note
nothing would now untwist: "You could take me out
and shoot me."
                 I call your name, faintly.
How can I, just to let you know I'm here,
jolt you back to all this - the milky drip-tube
feeding a congested sleep, the steely ambush
of clinical apparatus? And this grey window?
The frilly white pinks that smiled at me on the station
are straggly and anaemic in the hospital jar.
The scissors had gone, I could not shorten the stems.
I prop my note against them. But who will read it?

Somewhere near home the February sky
shows a bright new sickle. A wish! Sharp as a needle
jumps to the magnet this wish jumps to you -
if I could frame it, and if it could find you.

Rooster

For Patricia Sheaffer (who set the subject)

We share the same name and, in a manner of speaking,
the same language though in her country there are
mailboxes, automobiles and elevators
that are lifts on our terrain.
And she goes a journey riding *on* a train -
which in our country would be fraught with dangers.
Like driving on the right. And, where our *garriages*
are carefully framed to rhyme with carriages,
be sure she neatly backs into her *gurrh razh*.

Over there the bird of dawning is the rooster
(fie on the shameless name used by the Brits!)
which name of theirs gives a delightful boost to
their native punning rhymsters and their wits,
who wonder if it's best to be a crow and
to roost or be a rooster and to crow
(but they dunno).

We're cousins, ethnographically speaking,
it must be the weather makes the difference.
Over there they figure life is what you make it,
their smiles express a genial confidence.
When you are introduced they do not fumble
but clasp your hand as if this could become
the friendship of a lifetime.
If you ask how do they do they are always just fine.
Your Brit wields an umbrella muttering *mustn't grumble*.

Cousins, and yet out there they would look me up and down -
well, down any way - and tell me I'd have to go.
And here the red tape measures out her stay relentless.
We shall have a friend less
when she goes home to roost, or perhaps to crow.

For An Australian Visitor

This is the bird that wakes me in the morning
all through the summer with his light "Cuckoo!" -
a call like a mocking caress, wooing the summer,

summer that's always wandering and waning
and never means to stay as it would with you
in the south where skies are blue and the days warmer.

Shall I ever hear his carefree note returning
in another year and my heart not stir for you
when the thrilling lyrebirds shall have lured you under,

remembering in spring how you stalked the country straining
your strange Australian ear for his light "Cuckoo!" -
the exotic unheard bird, the northern wonder?

Intoxications

I

As he reels down the street the lamp-posts sway
though he does his best to steady them,
and people he wants to meet edge out of his way
though he calls out to them the friendliest of greetings.

He walks through a night of his own with more moons in it
than anyone else has, and pulsating rhythms
that nudge him into song - the world's a stage
that widens and contracts about his act.

II

Head down, intent, she burrows along the street
like a mole hollowing out a private darkness.
Observing no-one, she reckons herself invisible.
Should anyone call her name, she'd start like a shot hare.

Corners are delicate: a chance encounter there
could break the thread of her mutterings, could topple
the delicate balance of a line or rhyme.
Poor harmless maundering addict - words are her tipple.

Clothes

Clothes are like money, pretty much, all energy-defying:
no-one can ever have enough, so there's no point in trying.

Far better to invest your wealth at Waterstone's or Blackwell's:
for what a suit would set you back you've poetry in sackfuls.

And poetry begins in bliss and ends, they say, in wisdom,
while cashmere thins and cotton frays, and permanence there is none.

Of course you'd dress up like a toff to knock around with princes
and mince and bow and force a grin although your dress-shoe pinches.

But poetry can liberate and fashion's an oppressor,
so I'm a snapper-up of books and not a snappy dresser.

Funny Hat

Some laughter is half admiration at least -
take Mrs Shilling's latest hat for Ascot,
or, "Fancy talking like that to the boss!"

And some, that isn't, makes us all feel kin.
Who doesn't look a fool in a paper hat
or have this trouble with street signs, road maps,
plastic packs that won't open, launderettes?

But the last laughter is superior laughter:
we know we have more sense, we'd spot the banana skin
in time, we'd not swig out of the finger-bowls
or startle the neighbourhood with that barbarous hat.

Like a wild teacosy stalking past the window
it half eclipsed her face. Nobody knew her
but everyone knew of her. Everyone talked
and laughed.

        And then one day the word went round
they'd broken down the door, and found her hanging.

Visitation

The house pulsates to these
eccentric energies,
the bathroom shimmers and breaks into song
and all along
the walls a scattered flotsam of books, boots,
files, fancy tonics, socks, typescripts
piles into drifts, shifts
like sifting dunes. A cyclone's
force has demolished the usual boundaries.

Its core, weightless
as the pause between two breaths,
opens, contains all space,
all speech, silence.

And now the centre shifts,
the scattered drifts
under the whirlwind stress
achieve compactness.
A stuttering briefcase
has its mouth stopped, strapped,
chairs, tables are stripped
of every encumbrance.

He is gone in a clap,
concentrated, set
on his star-flecked progress
up to Olympus, no less.

The place below lies
diminished, breathless,
restored to trimness.
Only faint essences
like incense lingering in
deserted sanctuaries
proclaim that in this house
he sang, and was.

A Voice Goes Missing

These half-deserted rooms drowsed in the care
of one whose voice, mild but inexorable,
resembled so the living it was impossible
not to be taken in until the final
chill revelation - "There is no-one here" -
and the usual reassurance about messages.
The incumbent meanwhile floating in sundrenched seas
deepened his tan, approved the ambience,
or rising from the surf like Ulysses
startled the tall blondes with his eloquence.

Back in raw Surrey the slow diligence
of spiders reigned draping the stiff silence.
Occasional lovers broke their fast to call -
some past year's vintage, faint to hear those tones,
they took their fix and vanished, leaving no names.
The same unhurried voice answered them all,
satisfied all, kept all callers at bay,
till thieves unlatched the silence one black day
and took their pick, encountering no resistance.
Who knows in what obscure captivity
or on what far plane his new forced subsistence -
caged, with a blanket thrown over him nightly,
or in some limbo of lost voices still
Saying lightly, "If you'll leave your number I'll
get back to you as soon as possible"?

Emeritus

The Emeritus Professor, close on seventy,
bronzed, alert, dispensing wisdom and poetry,
never at a loss or unable to raise a smile,
is popular on the circuit, his affable easy style
charming the campus rabble of admiring young,
who find him an excellent fellow (although not one
for triflers perhaps or takers of liberties
with the English language in any of its modalities)
and a regular wandering star, whose light's half shed
in strange cold places, hoar frost mantling his head,
older than galaxies - no-one surmising at all
that in London, England, someone could still recall
with nostalgic smiles his laughter, some of his small
intimate gestures, his crazy habit of singing in bed.

The New Endymion

Moon, eerie visitant,
Earth-transfiguring light patrolling the sky,
distorting the waves' reach,
that you could be ever known as this world's known -
the thought was crazy.

But I wanted no urging on that insensate voyage,
hour after hour ploughing the furrowless sky
though my heart was ice
when you moved toward us, mute, in awful brightness
stepping out of the night.

Yet you received us, coolly, after your kind,
but graciously, let us roam and take our fill
of wandering, marvelling, plundering
where you lay still,
uneclipsed by shadow, naked even of air.

Lumbering, half-buoyant there,
we got by heart mood and contour and texture,
chronicling each feature,
then turned away abruptly, shipping a rare
collection of trophies, taking leave for ever.

And so home to the cocktails and the small talk
in a world I thought I knew:
"Well, that old moon we all go on thinking so romantic
up there will be just, for you,
a dusty place on the map at the end of a hard voyage."

I catch your image,
elate, virgin silver, remote now from my heart
as the stars you move among,
and scour the wastes of my mind trying for that smart
nonchalant answer I know will never come.

A Very Ordinary Life

Grew up when there were green fields
showing beyond the houses,
sat on a bench in school, learnt
rigour of boards and benches.
Soldiered for king and country;
toiled for the girl he wanted;
married with always scant means,
always to be augmented.
Sundays he dug the garden,
put up shelves or pictures the neighbours
admired in moderation.
He wasn't a thinking man
and he didn't think much of religion.
"Any afterlife I have,"
he said, "I'll live in my children."

Retired with a modest house,
survived on a modest pension,
kept up the drains and paintwork
and never neglected the garden.
Sundays he'd polish the car
ready for weekday shopping,
take the wife for a spin
out to Hainault or Epping.
He never had seen a Monet
and wouldn't have known a Turner,
but he always admired a sunset
or a pond with ducks in the corner.

What he felt no-one asked him,
what he thought no-one minded,
when he died no-one noticed
but the few he left behind him.
Even the doctors yawned,
his symptoms were so unexciting.

So where's the point of it all?
When he dropped serene and mellow
was it a hero's life he'd lived
or the life of a garden marrow?
One thing's sure and clear -
he'd never have troubled his wit
to answer such a conundrum.
His last words were, "Well, dear,
's been a fair old life. There's a bit
put by for you and the children."
And a well-stocked garden.

Moonlight

Moonlight unstrung things: when it reached the full
the wolves would get to howling inside my head.
Sometimes they'd snarl, then nothing would hold them.
That's where love ended.

Some men, when it's all over, walk away
or throw the girl out. That was not my custom.
"You gave me a good time," I used to say;
"I'll give you house room."

And I was in building, hot on renovation,
had the knowhow and the kit.
I don't suppose the moon ever looked in on
so snug a fit.

Each one had her place. I'd call to them by name
softly from the stairs, "We had some good times, right?
And what happened that last time - you know I never
meant it. Sleep tight."

But now the spies are scrabbling in chimney and wall,
unsettling everything, scattering dust.
The moon stares like a stranger. Things are all
coming unfocused.

Coniston Water

In Coniston Water the shadows lie deep;
at their root pale mouths fumble and flutter,
and pale is the secret they promised to keep
in Coniston Water.

Seven years in a life and the essences seep
clean away - not a grain of this mortal
frame's the same as that day when we made the waves leap
in a perilous quarter.

Seven threes have washed over us, live and dead. Steep
is the road to her bed, where they caught her.
Can these be the hands still that rocked her asleep
on Coniston Water?

The Lady Talks

The trouble is, once you hold the seat of power,
people think you're all-powerful, every disaster's
laid at your door, as if you could have stopped it.
He'd been his country's saviour, turned the tide
of battle for us. So on the old man's demise
(that was a nasty business) I encouraged him
for the good of the country to take charge of things.
He was the people's hero, and next of kin
in a manner of speaking: the sons had disappeared,
no-one knew where they'd gone. Some people thought
they'd killed the old man. They'd have had the motive.
It looked bad that it happened in our house, though.
And then that party! When his best friend failed us
and we heard what had happened, my poor husband
quite lost his head, saying he'd seen the man's ghost.
You can't think how unnerving those things are,
how in the long run they shake public confidence.
Leaders of men ought not to be so sensitive.
It was the last straw when that wretched woman
and her poor children - no, I can't bear to say it,
I do so feel for them, I have nightmares still.
And now our ungrateful people ... all these rumours!
I tell him, no need to worry. You know, he went
and got his fortune told, and they assured him
nothing could happen - they put it rather oddly -
nothing, they said, until the trees of the forest
should come marching against us. Well, you'd think
that ought to have made him happy. Trees don't walk.

Alcestis - The Inside Story

One thing I'll tell you : stay clear of gods and supermen,
and especially clear of anyone the gods
in their high simplicity think they can befriend.

That first summer he came to call on my father,
tipsy with confidence (no-one ever denied
Admetus anything - outright) he had his answer,
flattering enough to a hero: "Right, the girl's yours,
when you can come to fetch her in a carriage
drawn by yoked boars and lions." That got rid of him.
Who would have thought he'd get the god Apollo
to help him cheat? He *came* with boars and lions.

There are worse husbands. That time he was ill
with the doctors shaking their heads, I felt (I think)
all that a good wife should. There were the children.
And I kept out of the way of his drinking friends
like that hulk Hercules, all fists and biceps.
And when the astounding news came that Apollo
had managed to strike a deal: anyone willing
to die for Admetus' sake could save Admetus,
(gods, of course, cannot die) I hoped that someone -
some slave perhaps, tired of his life and canny,
whose children might become freedmen - would be found.

But no, it had to be someone in the family;
and you should have seen Admetus' face when first
his father then his mother declined the bargain,
dragging their rickety lives out to the last breath.
What must I do? My children fatherless?
Motherless? Which was worse? In any case
what would life be, after, if I had not offered?
What less could a loving wife do? What less a husband
than refuse such an offer? He did not refuse.
Staggering off to be with his grief alone,
he let me sink. Yes, he implored the gods
(too late) beating his breast, begging them all
To spare this paragon of wifely duty.

After which, Hades was a haven - if only
I could have stayed. However, in all the hubbub
indispensable to a properly run bereavement,
enter my husband's old friend Hercules
stopping by on his way to tame some horses.
Hospitality in all well-run houses
requires the activities of undertakers
to be kept from the guest. Admetus put a bold face on.
But in time the strong man, noticing all the wailing,
sensed something amiss. The servants told him nothing.
At last, half bleared (they say) he forced it out of them.
Then up he starts and flings away the cup,
swearing not Pluto nor Persephone
shall frustrate this exploit. And off he strides.

So here I am. What no doctor could do
this blundering oaf did. Now the old pair, both
glad enough then to let their son be ransomed,
looking at me see always the blank reproach
of what they refused. Admetus looks away.
A wife who's bought a man's life with her own
is a saint, dead; alive, an embarrassment.
There are the children. They look at me strangely -
to return from the dead is the last eccentricity.
Hercules no-one mentions. Save us from supermen!
That way we'll die just once, which is a sufficiency.

Return to Ithaca

As the keel scraped home on stony Ithaca
a shudder swept the islands; all the rich tapestry
of caves and palaces, whirlpools and citadels
was rolling away. The roar and pounce of the waves
lulled to a rumour as the path wound inland.
Outside the town a heap of common refuse
seemed stirring into life. "Argos!" he cried.
But the scrawny shape that urged itself towards him,
quivering a mangy tail, whimpering for joy,
had spent its strength. And still Ulysses climbed
to where the riotous princes, never thinking
vengeance so close, would stagger, choking in blood,
and slaves must purify the place of slaughter.

Then quiet came back, patterned with summer voices,
grassy whisperings, chuckles in the reed-bed,
and the lean dialect of crickets, so haunting
to fraught voyagers on their heaving plain,
nothing the sirens sang ever came near it.
And in the house astonishment had made dumb
long they sat, Penelope and her wanderer,
revolving memories - the long siege in Troy,
the landfall made, always to make again,
the weaving each night craftily unwoven
in the sad hall, holding at bay the bickering princes.

The crickets had gone silent; the fire glowed fainter;
shadows, stealing together, merged in one.
Sleep hovered near, words were falling away,
but each knew the alphabet of the other's heart.
He might have lifted the covers from her loom
and found she had woven the pale lotus-eaters,
the sea-nymph's girdle, Circe's treacherous cup,
the lumbering giant robbed of his one eye,
six-headed Scylla, or that sea-haunted cave -
Calypso's - and would not have been amazed.

She Questions Him

Come over into the light and tell me it all again -
that bit about the Cyclops scrunching up all those men,
the way you tricked him telling him you were called No-one,
and how you're the one man living that heard the sirens' song.
And that nymph who lent you her girdle. And what was it you say
all those years on Calypso's island, stopped you from getting away?
And who was the girl with the laundry, a princess you say and young,
who washed the brine from your dewlaps and wanted you for her own?
And that scheming hustler Circe enticing you into her den,
and all those wistful pigs you magicked back into men -
but how is it none of those sailors ever came home again?

If you want to know what I think, time-weathered wanderer, look -
if you're not the world's great hero, perhaps you should write a book.

Voice From The Labyrinth

So they put me in here, well out of everyone's way.
Queens should have issue in the royal line, not
these awkward hybrids, losers in the race,
inept at skills our urgent age has need of.

Solitude. Yes, well, you get used to it,
and every so often there were human voices,
young people - sent to join me, you might suppose.
Their alien intonations woke the echoes

and died. The silence thickens, air grows colder.
Now if I bellow through these cavernous wastes,
who's there to listen? Now if I take this flint
and scratch my crumbling history on these walls,

who will come and read? Is anyone out there still
living? Perhaps they've all abandoned Earth,
cocooned in weightlessness, probing through space
in quest of some dim half-hospitable planet,

time like a cheap clock running always slower,
history a text grown indecipherable,
the galaxies drifting further out of hail
and all this life a dream. And none to dream it.

The Minotaur Explains

You can say, if you like, I was misunderstood.
I'd call it something worse. In the first place,
that's not how the teeth go: men are carnivores,
cannibals even; bulls won't touch the stuff.
So all that about sacrificial maidens
and young men - you can stow it. They died of course,
of starvation mainly, wandering in the labyrinth.
There was grass, but grass is not the diet of humans.
The king wanted his wife's son out of the way,
and tales like that warned off the curious.
Besides, he liked doing nasty things to Athens.
Yes, I know Theseus came out of the labyrinth
waving his sword and saying he'd struck my head off.
But you know Theseus: is he the sort of man
whose word you'd trust? Remember Ariadne.
No, I'm still here. Why not call in and see?

Unicorn

Day after day I fed that unicorn
and when the earth lay quiet under the stars,
stooping by dank hedges and misty hollows,
I'd try for spells to bind his world to ours.

Sometimes I'd watch him bathed by the full moon
like something in a tapestry or dream.
All night he'd stand there, milk-white, unmoving
twinned by his shadow, no-one minding him.

The year grew late, and I piled stone on stone
building a byre to shield him from the cold
when fields are barren and the long nights come,
and spun a line tighter than spiders' thread,

that grips its mount when wind unseats the leaves,
in hope to hold him safe and bring him home.
But then a fiercer tremor shook the trees,
he stirred, shimmered like chiffon and was gone.

The Unicorn Speaks

They tell me I don't exist.
"You're only a figment," they say,
"of someone's imagination.
You'd better just go away."

Real, unreal - who decides?
Tell me this if you know:
whose heart beats for a friend's friend
as it beats for Romeo?

And who's more real to you -
your forebears over the hills
or the old man of La Mancha
harrying windmills?

But I grow faint with age,
and is the chance so small
I'm only part of a dream
and don't exist at all?

There's still a girl somewhere
glides through a dim château
who took my head in her lap
hundreds of years ago
and soothed away the wildness.
I dare say she would know.

Here Be Dragons

Everyone knows of the mythical rhinoceros
standing four-square in his massive armour plating.
Dürer has done his picture.

And the men Othello saw whose heads did grow
beneath their shoulders - other travellers saw them -
must have looked like gorillas.

Centaurs too, men so perfectly matched to their horses
they moved as one and passed for an entity,
seemed to have grown that way.

Then what do we make of dragons? Komodo ones
give bites that poison, wait for their prey to die,
hunt in packs, soft-paced, stealthy.

But real dragons, we learn, breathed fire, had wings
like giant umbrellas, ravaged the land solo,
bellowed, terrorised cities.

Reports differ on details: a number of them
seem half serpents. Their portraits in the Gallery
reveal serious discrepancies.

One single species, moon-blanched, rapier-horned,
the bestiaries' gentleman, is consistent. Yes, you
know where you are with unicorns.

THE WORLD WE LIVE IN AND BEYOND

A Bus Journey

A Nepalese girl graceful as a dancer
smiles, at the bus stop, then asks me my age.
I respond in kind, uncertain if that's the move
I'm meant to make. Is the question only proper
as a tribute to conspicuous seniority?

Our local buses serve an under-class -
housewives, immigrants, paupers, pensioners -
and, as you see in old Egyptian friezes,
these are far smaller than the important people,
a principle not lost on the designers
of seating for the masses. Crammed together,
we soon get chatting. A Bangladeshi matron
asks me, "How many children?" And then, "Why?"
Then my turn to ask. The answer sounds like "Eight".
Good heavens! Four such women could fill a classroom.
And grandchildren - ought I to ask that too?
At the next stop a Jamaican neighbour
gets on and questions me on where I'm going
and what I'm planning to do. (I think how lucky
it's nothing devious.) Must I return the question?

Finally comes and snuggles next to me
an indigenous Brit. Now we can talk of safe things
like the weather, the rising cost of stuff in Sainsbury's
and what she's getting her grandchildren for Christmas.

A Faint Celebration of London

I don't say it's a paradise. The jolting bus drags on its
pilgrimage to some far-off shrine, some centre fraught with promise.

The window's just a muddy blur but shows you nonetheless
rows of shopfronts in varying styles of dingy garishness.

Then as you reach the hub of things congestion's ten times worse,
you'll find you could have got along much faster in a hearse.

So have no truck with transport there. Leap out, take to your feet,
with fists and elbows slash your way along the seething street.

Make for some gallery, entrance free, the city's joy and pride;
quiet and spaciousness could all be there for you inside.

The whole world's choicest artefacts are on display for you,
if you can muscle in and get an unimpeded view.

But when there's an uncrowded room and you can rest, apart,
hordes of rampaging young rush through, brought here to study art.

Perhaps there'll be a bench somewhere to ease your bones. What bliss!
Hold it! The competition's fierce for any space like this.

Well, there are parks, the city's lungs. The world goes flocking there
to seek a little solitude and breathe untainted air.

I dream of some deserted beach washed by a quiet tide,
I dream of clean Venetian streets, clear and uncitified,

or airy Cumbrian fells where I went tramping young and strong.
But scruffy stuffy London's still the place where I belong.

Incident on a Train

All of us here must have somewhere to get to
eventually, but for most of us, here and now,
there's no hurry for that. The couple opposite
must fancy themselves at home on their own sofa
with no-one around to notice what they're at.
And a woman is plying her mobile with prodigal gestures
that might have had a meaning for somebody
far out of view, but are wasted on the rest of us.

And some have their crossword, digital game or book
or are lost in a dream, till right at the end of the carriage
a voice is suddenly raised and we turn to look
at a woman screeching about the doom in store for us
who are frittering away our minutes, our thoughtless lives,
not heeding the gospel, never seeing the light.
A blight is settling down on the lot of us,
we can't think where to look in our misery,
till a rough male voice breaks into the flow of indictment
shouting, "Sod off!" and restores bonhomie.

Keeping an Eye on the Thames

It was the Thames, you told me, and not the seaside
glinting below the wall we turned our backs on
as we climbed up steps and steps to the echoey galleries,
shrines where great paintings blessed their worshippers.
And afterwards a giant grandfather clock
loomed up, that had a boy's name. There was Parliament,
a very special place, they made the laws there.

The wheel has turned, and art's now all the rage;
crowds throb through galleries, surge over bridges,
each year more teeming and more turbulent.
Even old Thames that used to lie so quiet
beside that building where they made the laws...
Come out to Charlton, see those silver helmets.
Those aren't the casques of submerged warriors;
those are the Barrier, primed against a river
minded to rear up and engulf us all.

Seeing in the Year

In earlier times they used to sound their hooters
at midnight on the Thames, a chorus of rapture
to welcome in the new year. Why so sure
new should mean better? Forecasts now are sadder;
the hooters don't do hooting any more.

Jollity could be voted out of fashion
this year. Of one thing we're all confident:
everything's going to go from bad to worse.
What longed-for, unimaginable event
could throw our grinding gears into reverse?

Let's face the new year with a bleak forecast;
that way no new mishap will catch us napping.
Pull a long face, put on your blackest black
and groan aloud. That way, whatever happens,
you'll find you did the right thing, looking back.

Kills 99%

You felt you'd got the whole thing in the bag,
from Eden on you never thought to doubt
Man was the measure of all things. That brag
gives you a hint of what I'm on about.

History, that has the lowdown on these things
from ages none of your lot can recall,
shows the whole pageant - islands, empires, kings -
everywhere swelling to dwindle, rising to fall.

You scrub and scour and steam, wield the spray gun,
gargle and floss, and cheerfully forget
it's high time those bacteria had their fun.
Our lightning changes may outfox you yet.

I am the hundredth germ. I am the One.

How Things Got This Way

The Devil used to gnash his teeth all day when I was young.
Idleness was his element, and there was almost none.

You had to get up in good time to start the morning right.
Before you put the kettle on there was the fire to light

with wood to chop and coal to fetch and newspaper to screw up,
and when you lit the pile and blew, it threatened to blow you up.

On Mondays when the washboard reigned with bluebag, starch
 and wringer
the work could go on all day long and even hold up dinner.

Evenings you'd turn the wireless on to sit down and relax,
always with something in your hands to knit or darn or patch.

And men when they were home from work, if they were listening too,
would sport a pipe or fag to show they'd something they could do.

Machines take on our old jobs now and leisure's all the rage;
the couch potato is a breed not bred before this age.

No-one writes letters, though a few will scribble on a card.
Mobiles replace all that; besides, spelling has grown too hard.

Old Nick can think of things to do; the hints come thick and fast:
Nothing to pay for eighteen months. Order now while stocks last.

Don't wait for those small luxuries. Go on, shop till you drop.
Who cares what you may be or do? What counts is what you've got.

All day he sidles up behind, crooning in stygian glee:
Dear technophiliac humankind, your tribe belongs to me.

The Aged - A Solution

One present cause of discontent being the lack of housing,
your enterprising government - you'll never catch us drowsing -
comes up with an expedient we think you'll find imposing.

Our problem's with the elderly, who keep on multiplying.
Just one can hog the space of three. You never see them trying
to move, and some apparently have lost the art of dying.

This state of things will hardly seem what our good public wishes.
House-blockers, like bed-blockers, must move on, with space so precious.
To shoot them, though, would be extreme, and utterly un-British.

So let's rent out a granny flat or some space we can pass on -
an outhouse, garage, who knows what, convenient for conversion.
It needn't take a lot of space to house an aged person.

And then we'll see you pensioners convert your homes to sterling.
Think of the fun that will be yours, the money you'll be earning,
the nice compact new premises where you'll wake up one morning.

You can't conceive how easily you'll find the means to manage
this uptodate, commitment-free and labour-saving ménage,
your superspecial minispace, stowed snug inside a garage.

Return of the Comet

A prime one this year, arriving prompt at evening,
a smudged radiance unsettling the skyline, a train
of old baggage, rocks, bricabrac, mementos
of the grand tour - who knows half where he's been?

Last visit, the Pharaohs were furbishing their tombs,
provisioning for the long inland voyage,
spruce with gold masks to smile for them and sway
the various gods of passage, the deep judges.

But here at the date of reunion the smile awaiting
recognition is a stranger's. These space-age affairs
are for types with strong hearts and long calendars, not
for wimps that will not wait three thousand years.

Science Will Tell You

Science will tell you what you ought to know
and when it speaks it's pointless to dispute it,
so when Professor Cox says time's an arrow
don't ask him if he knows who chanced to shoot it

or ask if arrows travel in a curve
sailing through space, since space is curved, they say,
and so the course might run and never swerve,
turning tomorrow into yesterday,

and circumnavigate heaven and persist
to add a new dimension to Big Bang
and by an age-old astrophysic twist
prove not an arrow but a boomerang.

Life History Of Stones

In the beginning there were stones,
in the stones, crevices,
intricate crystals organising themselves,
achieving a vividness.

Then a quickening, a new inflection
in the unending question
propounding itself, the aboriginal Word
inscribing itself in the rocks.

A flash, and it had come,
the quite unpredictable
lurch in the hurrying clock,
the first pulsating cell - my parent and yours.

All nature ran amok
rioting in sap and flesh,
but the stones went on quietly
being their stony selves.

In them the atoms danced, innocent minerals
congregated in silence,
and the lichens laboured raising their green and russet
out of the dust,

energy begetting energy; but
no urge or aspiration ever troubled
the blank sleep of the stones,
their sturdy singleness.

When the last branch is withered,
the last sea dead,
and when the last wind comes,
what will be there but stones?

Creation and After

First there was mind.
But mind's hardly mind without
something to think about.

"Atoms," it thought,
and right away appeared
electrons dancing in patterns.

Dances of the dead.
Mind wanted something more.
"Surprise me," it said.

There was a flourish.
Sap rose in a green world
all set to nourish

life that spawned, throbbed,
barbarous in tooth and claw.
No truce in that war.

Life, yes. But mind
kept looking for something
of its own kind.

He came, god-shaped,
lobbying with clamorous prayers
the gods he aped.

When he asked, "Why?"
all arts, all sciences
were his to try.

Now it's "Why not?"
Now he'll recast the world,
manage the lot.

Then there'll be only mind
if mind can still make out
long after nothing's left
to think about.

Origin

"You can't have God *and* Darwin." A mere spark
started off life and that's it, they aver.
It's one blind struggle: what succeeds survives,
mutates, spawns, in a mechanical mindless blur.

Yes, well, there are the fossils, the DNA,
the mighty mathematical universe,
the relentless dance of atoms, the jubilee
of rioting plant-life. I have to agree of course.

Then, count the genes, I'm half a daffodil
or nearly so, which I delight to find.
I admire the ingenuity of it all,
the design you tell me can't have been designed.

But what force took my hand and moved my pen,
prompted those lines in the poem? What, no-one, ever,
to thank for trees, sleep, streams, that blackbird singing,
this table in the sun, our day together?

Space Is The Playground Of The Illusionist

Those spangles in the sky that look like stars
are not all genuine. You can't use perspective
to tell you which of them are really blazing,
which are imposters, flaunting borrowed fire,
and which, for all the pace they travel at,
are tardy messengers, so long on the journey
the senders have folded and gone. Are we deceived
when we see stars that aren't there any more
although their light still travels and is here?

Rainbows too, that shifty lot, tricks of the light,
we see them, yes, but are they really there?
And what of that arch-illusionist, the moon
whose dreary dusty wastes we think we know,
and yet those dream-like hauntings still surprise us,
transfigure the world as palpably as snowfall,
and move in us like tides. The light's purloined
but whose then is the magic? There are stars too
that flicker on screens, draw tears from us and laughter,
but have no being. And great poets disappear
behind their lines, becoming illusions somewhere.

Rainbow

Nothing to hear, and no-one saw it come.
But there it was, like something out of a book,
making no pretence of realism, bowing over the washed fields
on points of wavering light. After the performance
it went as it had come, slyer than Banquo's ghost,
leaving a wide absence but with meaning in it.

Yes, it was just a trick of the light, and done
with prisms. But that sense of absolution,
a stay of oppression from old habits of being,
(how Noah must have felt it, out of the bestial closeness!)
old greyness scoured miraculously with light -
is that less, or more, real? As we are ourselves real,
who will agitate the air a little longer,
round whose eventual vanishing absolving atoms will
without a word spoken rearrange themselves.

The Snake's Version

He could set the scene all right, I grant you that;
ours was a prime one, Monty-Don-type stuff,
fully equipped with arbours, fountains, fruit-trees,
glades, grottos, winding streams, dovecotes - in fact
a small menagerie, all in perfection. Still,
perfection's stagnation, that I could have told him.
He had this pair of leads; the rest of us
just got supporting roles. That's favouritism.
No-one loves favourites. And these were paragons,
supposed to start a family, get things going.
But they were so perfect they never had a clue,
spent all day gardening and admiring each other.
I thought they were missing out on a lot of fun
and it wouldn't hurt to give a jolt to the plot.

There was this fig tree he said not to touch.
(All that kerfuffle wasn't just for an apple.)
The figs were perfect, luscious, bursting-ripe,
and I told those greenhorns no, he'd never miss them,
just put them there to spark off enterprise,
though (as it happened) those figs were all for him;
he'd go there every day to watch them ripening.
Well, gods when they lose their rag don't act like angels,
they go berserk. He booted them into the world,
penniless immigrants with no place to stay.
It wrings your heart. Makes a good story though.
Like I said, the gaffer could set the scene all right
but no head for a plot. I helped him there.

The Wrong Kind of Apple

In those dark days there were no gardening manuals
to help a pair of greenhorns starting out.
They'd never know their Coxes from their Bramleys,
and all of horticulture lay in doubt.

So when he slithered up hinting politely
(as an old hand who knew a thing or two)
his willingness to help them, it seemed likely
they'd learn what they could have, what they must do.

A strange location smiles when you've good neighbours.
He showed them haunts they'd never known were theirs
and trees undreamed of, fruits of many flavours.
They helped themselves, there always would be spares.

And one he told them would be good for healing.
(He knew to a tittle what he was about.)
It was a cider apple and sent them reeling
in the cool of the day, and got them both slung out.

What Now?

All through my childhood he was sitting up there
seeing everything we did. It would go on record.
(Handy that tagging with the double helix.)
But now the whole show's just a dance of atoms,
though no-one asks how atoms learnt to dance
in the beginning when the heavens and earth
rose out of chaos. After which everything

(they tell us) fell out quite unsupervised,
letting some forms survive, supposed the fittest,
with man supremely conscious lord of all this.
He ate the fruit of knowledge rind and core,
revamped the world so he could take it over
and when the ransacked world turned sick and sour
looked for some other planet he could conquer.

But Earth can breed avengers of her own
and microbes learn to outmanoeuvre humans,
at any moment something stressed explodes
and outraged seas assert their reclamations.
Materialists may have to face about:
the likelihood's that mind is everywhere
masquerading as matter. Better look out!

The Takeover

"Look, God," said the Newstyle Monkey,
"you made the universe. Right?
And a pretty impressive job. I can honestly say
we all appreciate it. Still, there are things...Take pain -
the trouble it's given us trying to put that right.
And I think you'll admit you started out with too many
slugs, bugs, rodents, vultures and other
unnecessary animals. And again, bringing in time,
that was a big mistake - everything coming undone,
having to be done again. Still, we're stuck with that,
and luckily we've come up with a few materials
you might call time-proof. But now that brings us
to the population question. That notion of yours -
be fruitful, multiply - worked all right at first
when the whole outfit was new, room aboard for everyone.
In this day and age, though...frankly, the original design
has got a bit out of hand. Still, not to worry
if it's getting too much for you. That's what we're here for -
world reclamation, disinfestation, sound exploitation -
it's all in the pipeline. What it comes down to is this...
Why don't you make the whole conglomeration
over to us - we've got the technology -
and sit on your arse?"
                        God was silent.
He didn't so much as blow his nose to show
he was wanting time to think.
                    "Well, Almighty,
isn't it a bit late now to be going it alone?

Like I said, we have the technology. Put it this way -
when did you ever come up with a design
that was mothproof, rustproof, rotproof? Things we invent,
are made to last. Take this watch on my wrist -
accurate to one second in a million years."

There was something like a laugh - not a polite one -
or more of a cough - the sky clearing its throat
or some such far-off primitive electric
manifestation. But in these times who's bothered
when a cloud turns sarcastic?

How To Be God - Just The Basics

To start with, you will need a calculator;
numbers must stay in balance, that's the first rule.
Then come the laws of physics, once thought fate or
a judgement. These, you'll find, are universal.
Still, let's take something simple - let us take a
small planet for our earliest rehearsal.
There's no scintilla of a chance you'll manage
if you can't cope there without doing damage.

Ecology comes next. If it's abhorrent
to let the hungry lion rend the deer,
the deer will multiply and strip the forests
and leave no vegetation anywhere.
Tallest trees too must totter, lose their promise,
rot and make way for new life to appear.
And mind the wasps have nectar, that gratuity
to keep them labouring in perpetuity.

With all these disparate species on the go, it
could be you'll find some joker in the pack
will turn things upside down before you know it.
Your system must be geared to things like that;
have your switch ready and be poised to throw it
before the world starts wondering what you're at.
Get a tornado, virus or mosquito
to do the business for you if you need to.

You ask what's to become of the Commandments
and favours shown to persons of true piety.
Ethics, like species, undergo amendments;
who's to judge what's what in all this variety?
And those apocalyptic world-derangements,
like fire and flood, have no care for society.
"But God is love," you say, "they taught that much to me."
No. Love's for us. He can't afford such luxury.

Off the Record

*So saying, with delight he snuffed the smell
Of mortal change on earth. (Paradise Lost X, 272-3)*

When the white blast "blew" the Far Galaxies -
such were the terms of Uriel's report -
"Off with you!" said the Gaffer. So, quick as thought,
we landed, Gable and Mike and I, who in these
investigative missions now always make one.

Whirlwinds of angry dust blotted the sun,
ash underfoot and darkness overhead.
We had to switch vision to infra-red,
peering to assess what damage had been done.
A blank - just blackened emptiness everywhere,

and silence. Nothing. We could only stare
dumbfounded. What did it? Nothing to show.
You might have thought some tiny spark or glow
would live to illumine all that was not there
of all that had been there once - was it so long?

The maestro built the place up like a song
out of some rhythm that ran in his head,
didn't stop by to listen much - instead,
thinking his score unlikely to go wrong,
tossed off an airy blessing and went his way,

leaving the tune to sing itself, you may say.
And as time passed and the great opus grew,
with always something somewhere else to do,
such schemes became the order of the day.
So here we stood, trying to puzzle out

what could have gone wrong this time. Well, no doubt,
if the natives hadn't become extinct, or fled,
we'd flush some of them out soon, live or dead.
We scrunched through heaps of cinders, spying about,
but could find nothing, neither tree nor beast,

till moving out, seeking where there was least
ruin, we found this shadow on a wall,
a kind of fossil, an aboriginal
called Adameve, once a vaunted masterpiece;
more of these; then the blackened carcases.

League upon league they were rotting - beasts, birds, trees.
"All yours!" said Gabriel, as if I hadn't known
long ago, from far away scenting my own.
Still, it shook me, having to take charge of all these.
But where was the other still waiting to be found?

"What other?" you ask. Well now, it can't be sound
sense to suppose a whole species immolated
itself, its home and everything created.
A likely story! Somewhere still around
we'd have to find the culprit, some late sport

of the evolutionary process - which, we thought,
on this planet had to be some superman
or super-reptile not in the maestro's plan,
with power to reduce original types to nought.
What we found gave a jolt to our reckoning.

Carapaced, yes, we'd met that kind of thing,
but curved, not with this angular symmetry.
Eyes, mouth, ears - no telling where they were meant to be,
nipples all sizes, valves shutting and opening,
intestines random as a tangle of bines -

clearly not based on any of our designs.
Yet these things lived, jabbered some harsh language,
performed some kinds of tasks, could flash with rage
or who knows what passions. Some talked in signs.
Some were perhaps not quite right in the head.

But they seemed infants still, it must be said,
sucking their life-stream from a cord in clear
independence of the surrounding atmosphere;
unplug the life-cord, they were instantly dead,
like all the other species round about.

They must have done the damage, there's no doubt.
Who else could? And though to my discerning breath
they smelt of nothing, neither life nor death,
they showed life's old relentless drive to out-
smart other forms. And here they were, supreme.

We left - no hurry could be too extreme -
to report back and apply for re-instruction,
not dreaming our tale would meet with the deduction
all we'd encountered must have been a dream.
"An ingenious invention," all agreed,

"but in real life how could such things succeed?"
"See for yourselves," we said. "Remember those isles
called Paradise once?" More incredulous smiles,
sardonic now, on all sides. "Look," we said. "Read."
All looked. And there was nothing on the files.

Announcement

Passengers of the 8.15, do not be alarmed.
Your train has been arrested in mid-journey.
This is no accident. Grills lowered
electronically on doors and windows
are for your safety. Please do not
attempt to emerge. Electrical currents
generated round this train would inflict
very severe burns. Have no anxiety
that you will not punctually reach your workplace
or other destination. No-one now awaits you.
This whole country is, to the uttermost,
in our protection. You are safe here.

We have given most strict consideration
to matters of hygiene: this train will daily
move one entire length along the line.
Daily nutrition will be served by robots
at window grills. Also we shall monitor
on closed circuit every carriage
and remove by overhead suction systems
any diseased or dead. You need have
no anxiety. Our agents have fully
researched all modern economic
and humane methods of stock management
in farms and laboratories on this planet.
We find such subjects on earth do best
in confined quarters. Scientific feeding,
airducts, lighting keep them contented.
Humbler species can thus contribute
to science and sustenance of higher beings.

So you will be managed, rest assured,
in best modern fashion with all improvements.
In course of time also light will be modified
to give tranquility. This is a recorded
announcement. It will be repeated.

Dinosaur

I had a brain at each end like the latest thing on a railroad
(though going backwards was never part of my plan)
and a mechanism for converting small birds into energy
and a three-mile wingspan.

When I preened my scales, legions of bats flew out of them,
when I sang in spring the fossils danced in the rocks.
I could make a snack of the mincing new-style wildlife
you see on the box.

The earth was mine. A season ticket on Concorde -
that's peanuts, man; wherever I clapped my wings
skies applauded. I sampled success all right
and all its trappings.

What went wrong? Now listen, homunculus erectus,
rearing up on your two hind legs to focus your wit
on the sprawling lesser species, success - well, you can have
too much of it.

A Fishy Theory

It was a queer old trout told me this one,
tippling in the Mermaid, trying to get our bearing
and a bit dazzled by the setting sun.

It goes like this. It seems there was this herring,
a bright young fellow, a bit uppity,
caused quite a stir beneath the waves declaring

there must be life on *land* as well as sea,
or what was land for? Something primitive,
without intelligence, most probably.

"But how'd it breathe? You have to breathe to live,
and breathing's done in water, that's well known,"
huffed one old herring. Neither side would give.

Just then a sort of shuddering, shifting moan
ran through the lot - a slithering, writhing huddle,
a hoisting into air of all as one.

They hated it - fish don't enjoy a cuddle.
But still the cords kept tightening round the haul:
they'd nothing left to breathe, not even a puddle.

And so they died, thus proving once for all
grand theories must expect a grand rebuttal:
life outside water - no, not possible.

And now I'm quite as dry as any cuttle-
bone, so let's sup and give up being subtle.

How To Know Vampires

A scream or a trail of blood may lead you to them,
or you may discern a fixity of speculation -
though in that case it could be late for reflection -
centred on the base of your throat.

With suspicious characters the safest course of action
is to catch them unawares with a good joke
or in any situation in which a smile or a gape
will be either involuntary or mandatory.

Try praising their hairdos or introducing them to royalty.
Engage them in chat and you may readily
mark those generic fangs that are such a giveaway
and take evasive action while you still may.

One clash of those jaws could dispatch you straight to hell -
though naturally only if you are already set on that course.
A danger with vampires is, absorbed in this curious
investigation you could overlook symptoms that may be serious.

Anyone can spot dental caries, blood pressure, obesity -
but just now in the dark, what was that involuntary
lunge? And that stain on your canines? And did the curve
of your lips slip from smile to snarl inadvertently?

A Letter To The Angel Of The North

Dear Sir, I have thought of you often, now that the nights are closing in,
standing out in that open landscape with so little clothing.
I have been in the North and know that their weather can be far from clement,
and I feel that in leafy Charlton with me you would be in your element.

I have read that angels are supposed to be largely creatures of fire,
though I would stress that that is by no means a quality I should require.
It is true I am a passionate woman but that is mostly for rhyme,
and I think you will find I have a positive penchant for the sublime.

Also I don't smoke or swear (in general) or drink - except for Earl Grey
and the occasional sip of wine when there's a wedding or a birthday.
And my modest proportions will fit in neatly under your wing -
which in these days of models like bean-poles you will agree is something.

It has to be said, though, I have seen a few more winters than you,
but experience is something an angel will have the wisdom to value.
And I have to admit I am anything but an A1 cook,
though I know all about the way to the heart being through the stomach.

But you, sir, I dare say, won't have such a thing as a stomach at all -
if you will forgive me this once for being so personal.
I know that you angels are really quite a superior breed,
but all my friends seem to think we should be well suited.

However, if you should decide against me considering all things,
perhaps you'd just let me knit you a muffler to keep out the cold these damp
        evenings.

Hermit Wanted

Dear Sirs, I see you are currently in need of a hermit.
I am a timeworn poet looking out for preferment.
You'll be wanting something more than a holy old curmudgeon
who'll skulk inside your grotto with never a thought of budging.
What you need is a bona fide bard who'll tramp to and fro
muttering his wayward fancies like poets long ago,
but shaggy, with unkempt beard, a cloak the size of a tent
and a rosary or some such appropriate accoutrement.

All these requirements I can guarantee to provide,
having rather, appearance-wise, tended to let things slide
since my last wife vanished in regrettable circumstances.
Your grotto, I trust, will have all the usual appurtenances -
ensuite, TV, a microwave, Broadband and space enough
for the stock of books and paper I'll need for writing my stuff.
Then your grotto, and tea-house, will - no question - rocket to fame.
Yours faithfully, Lancelot Wildeve. (Not, of course, my real name.)

The Great Leap

You can die of ladybirds: one settled on my cousin,
a young woman of blameless reputation
who was keeping company with Giles Reddipin
the entomologist. They were down by the river
when they took a jolt hearing the tweedy accents
of Aunt Azalea his sole relative
striding their way. "What ho, young Giles!" she boomed
confidentially. "I thought it would be a kindness
to let you know you can be seen from the road."
My cousin stared: "I had thought her kind extinct."
She meant Azalea, not the ladybird,
which was taking off, but Giles gave a great leap
to retrieve this specimen. The town heard the splash
as he hit the water. The ladybird got away
but it was the end of the line for the Reddipins.
Everywhere you find nature siding with insects.

The Snowdrop's First Assignment

When disgruntled woolly mammoths
trumpeted across the snowfields
waking God up with the racket,
saying what a bore the snow was,
saying, "Can't you send more fodder?"
he resolved to quell the riot
promising things would be better.
But they knew about such answers,
thumped the bearer of the letter.

Then he got his aides together,
told his troubles in a whisper.
They went at it hell for leather
working out a proper system.
Finally they got the thing done.
"This will keep the blighters quiet.
Tell them we've invented springtime."

But the mob just wouldn't buy it.
"Yes," they said, "a likely story!
All we get from you are winters.
Best be quick or you'll be sorry.
Send some miracle. Convince us."
Heaven's in a great quandary.
Someone has to think of something
soon, or the balloon will go up.
Thumbs are twirling, heads are thumping -
such a humming and harrumphing!
Then they got it: sent the snowdrop.

The Sad Case Of The Fractals

A nonsense poem. Some wag at a workshop had proposed Fractals as the subject for the next poem. The word had not then got into the dictionaries and I assumed that, like so many intractable terms that were giving me grief at the time, it must be something to do with computers.

The fractals are wringing their digits -
you never did see such a sight.
They are raising emaciated manuals
and twisting their pedals with fright.

You may order the whole start-up menu
but the cursor will lead you a dance;
though you've full microjustification
still, old apple, you don't stand a chance.

They have set every toggle switch twitching,
they have tabset and scrolled with their might,
but the fractals have met with destructals
and now nothing will ever come right.

Horace Updated

*After **Diffugere nives** (Odes IV.7)*

The snow's all finished, grains begin to sprout,
and soon we'll need to get the Flymo out.
The floods are gone, that old forecaster's bane
that had us rushing out to poke the drain.

What a relief to all this change of scene is,
and how the young will flaunt their new bikinis!
But nothing lasts. Summer will come, and then
autumn, and then it's winter back again.

When winter comes, it gums up everything.
It's not just that the birds forget to sing;
this deathly touch that chills us through and through
puts us in mind of what we always knew:

that - heron, human or hippopotamus -
Death's out there gunning for the lot of us.
Live while you can, or you could well regret it.
Spend and enjoy; don't let the taxman get it.

Whether you're Mother Teresa or some hood,
once you're put underground you're gone for good.
You may have kept, or broken, all the laws;
no bribes or barristers can plead your cause.

Moses, Houdini, Martin Luther King,
Keats, Crippen, Hitler, Elvis and Marilyn,
they're all down there, dismissed with no appeal.
It's FINIS, and you can't run back the reel.

Index of Titles

A Celebration: for A.J. 47
Aged - A Solution, The 136
Alcestis - The Inside Story...115
Anniversary..89
Announcement 155
Another Autumn...25
As If iii
Autumn Takes Over 66
"Backward"..4
Blacking the Range..3
Bus Journey, A 129
Cinema of the Thirties..13
Climbing Cader Idris..78
Clothes 102
Coniston Water...113
Creation and After..140
Dialogue with Plum Tree 93
Dinosaur...157
Door Onto The Street, A 19
Emeritus 107
Encounter 55
End of the Line...30
Ever Gracious Minister, The 40
Exit a Princess..91
Faint Celebration of London, A 130
Fishy Theory, A..158
Floribunda 20
For An Australian Visitor 100
For Audrey in May...48
Frog In Ivy 58
Funny Hat...103
George Claessen Nearing Ninety...86
Gifts From The Garden 26

Going To The Polls	41
Grandpa, A	6
Grass	76
Great Leap, The	162
Headland, The	32
Heart's-Ease	17
He Comes Back	94
Here Be Dragons	125
Hermit Wanted	161
Home, A	53
Horace Updated	165
Horticultural Question, A	65
How Things Got This Way	135
How To Be God - Just The Basics	150
How To Know Vampires	159
Ice	34
Identities	84
In a Summer Garden	61
In Aunt Mona's House	92
Incident on a Train	131
Inhospitable Place, An	38
In Praise Of Summer	62
In Time Of Elm Sickness	70
Into the Depths	75
Intoxications	101
Islands	64
Jays on the Lawn	59
Keeping an Eye on the Thames	132
Kills 99%	134
Lady Talks, The	114
Late Friendship, A	96
Letter to the Angel of the North, A	160
Life History Of Stones	139
Look At It This Way	15
Millbank Steps	87

Minotaur Explains, The	122
Moonlight	112
My Father's War	10
New Endymion, The	108
New Neighbour	56
No Flowers	22
Noises in the Night	5
Not a Letter	23
No Transmission	35
Off the Record	152
Old Man Comes for Christmas, The	36
Origin	142
Owls	71
Poetry He Said	24
Possessor of a Toothpick, The	39
Prayer for Hallowe'en	18
Question for Descartes, A	85
Rainbow	144
Rainy Day In The Strand	27
Remembering B.W.	95
Return of the Comet	137
Return to Ithaca	118
Robin and Rake	68
Rooster	98
Sad Case of the Fractals, The	164
Science Will Tell You	138
Seeing in the Year	133
Series Discontinued	31
She Questions Him	120
Sisters in a Wood	33
Snake's Version, The	145
Snowdrop's First Assignment, The	163
Sonnet for a Stranger	21
Space Is The Playground Of The Illusionist	143
Spool Runs Back, The	8

Spring In The City	60
Sunday Afternoon Walk	28
Takeover, The	148
Tale of Mud, A	12
Talking of Travel	42
Telling the Time	9
The Sea	74
Three Birthday Poems	48
To a Blue Butterfly	57
Touch of Earth, The	72
Tracking Down 4B	44
Trafalgar Square	14
Trafalgar Ward	37
Tree, A	77
Under the Clock	16
Under The Leaves	63
Unicorn	123
Unicorn Speaks, The	124
Unremarkable Day	46
Very Ordinary Life, A	110
Visitation	104
Voice From The Labyrinth	121
Voice Goes Missing, A	106
Voyage of Discovery	45
Water in its Phases	73
What Now?	147
Which Portrait Painter?	83
Winter Coming	67
"Woman Reading"	29
Work	11
Wrong Kind of Apple, The	146
Zero	69

Printed in Great Britain
by Amazon